T0318456

The Neuroscience of Multimodal Persuasive Messages

In this book, Dirk Remley applies his model of integrating multimodal rhetorical theory and multi-sensory neural processing theory pertaining to cognition and learning to multimodal persuasive messages. Using existing theories from multimodal rhetoric and specific findings from neurobiological studies, the book shows possible applications of the model through case studies related to persuasive messages such as those found in political campaign advertising, legal scenarios, and general advertising, including print, videos, and in-person settings. As such, the book furthers the discussion of cognitive neuroscience and multimodal rhetorical theory, and it serves as a vehicle by which readers can better understand the links between multimodal rhetoric and cognitive neuroscience associated with persuasive communication in professional and educational environments.

Dirk Remley is Professor in the Department of English at Kent State University, USA. He is the author of How the Brain Processes Multimodal Technical Instructions, Baywood 2015 and Exploding Technical Communication, Baywood 2015.

Routledge Studies in Technical Communication, Rhetoric, and Culture
Series Editors: Miles A. Kimball and Charles H. Sides

For a full list of titles in this series, please visit www.routledge.com.

This series promotes innovative, interdisciplinary research in the theory and practice of technical communication, broadly conceived as including business, scientific, and health communication. Technical communication has an extensive impact on our world and our lives, yet the venues for long-format research in the field are few. This series serves as an outlet for scholars engaged with the theoretical, practical, rhetorical, and cultural implications of this burgeoning field. The editor welcomes proposals for book-length studies and edited collections involving qualitative and quantitative research and theoretical inquiry into technical communication and associated fields and topics, including user-centered design; information design; intercultural communication; risk communication; new media; social media; visual communication and rhetoric; disability/accessibility issues; communication ethics; health communication; applied rhetoric; and the history and current practice of technical, business, and scientific communication.

The Neuroscience of Multimodal Persuasive Messages

Persuading the Brain

Dirk Remley

Routledge
Taylor & Francis Group

LONDON AND NEW YORK

First published 2017 by Routledge

2 Park Square, Milton Park, Abingdon, Oxfordshire OX14 4RN
52 Vanderbilt Avenue, New York, NY 10017

Routledge is an imprint of the Taylor & Francis Group, an informa business

First issued in paperback 2019

Library of Congress Cataloging-in-Publication Data

Names: Remley, Dirk, author.
Title: The neuroscience of multimodal persuasive messages:
persuading the brain / by Dirk Remley.
Other titles: Routledge studies in technical communication,
rhetoric, and culture.
Description: New York: Routledge, [2017] | Series: Routledge
studies in technical communication, rhetoric, and culture |
Includes bibliographical references and index.
Identifiers: LCCN 2017001429 |
Subjects: LCSH: Persuasion (Psychology) | Cognitive
neuroscience. | MESH: Persuasive Communication | Cognitive
Neuroscience Classification: LCC BF637.P4 |
NLM BF 637.P4 | DDC 153.8/52—dc23
LC record available at https://lccn.loc.gov/2017001429

ISBN: 978-1-138-63581-4 (hbk)
ISBN: 978-0-367-88834-3 (pbk)

Typeset in Sabon
by codeMantra

Contents

List of Figures

Permission Page

For figure 5.1

1 Persuasive Rhetoric and the Brain

Rhetorical Choices in Multimodal Persuasion

Why are politicians always smiling in political campaign advertisements? Why are adorable babies included in such photographs and photo-opportunities? Why do candidates seem to integrate the ugliest photo of their opponent while using black and white for the photo instead of color? Why do advertisers seem to integrate babies in advertisements for products or services that have no relationship to babies, such as in vehicle ads? Why do automobile manufacturers use attractive men, women, and families in their advertisements when they are trying to sell a vehicle? All of these are rhetorical choices marketers make in an effort to persuade the viewer toward certain action. Marketers know that nothing is included or excluded from a commercial accidentally; everything in the commercial or advertisement is there for a reason. Answers to all of these questions are easily found in scholarship related to the neuroscience of persuasion and the rhetoric of persuasion. This book attempts to mix the two sets of scholarship toward a unifying theory of persuasive multimodal rhetoric and practice.

To do this I use a model I introduced in another book, *How the Brain Processes Multimodal Technical Instructions*, refining that model and advancing its application. The model combined neuroscience scholarship with scholarship about multimodal rhetoric and instructions and cognition. Cognition is generally defined to include perception and understanding of the world as well as learning and comprehension. Persuasion involves one's perception of a given situation; so, this book considers persuasion relative to an audience's perception.

Politicians have consultants to help them plan their political messages for the best rhetorical effect. Marketers look for any means by which to persuade an audience toward action, and there is a growing body of research on how certain rhetorical choices affect audiences' perception, right down to the color of a product or facial expression of a child in the commercial or advertisement. Attorneys who are involved with court proceedings and jury trials also have a body of research upon which to draw to understand who their jury, or audience, is. An attorney must understand as much of the demographic and psychographic makeup of a given jury pool as possible. Many attorneys will encourage clients to settle out of court and avoid trial, because an out-of-court settlement may be more favorable than the outcome of a jury trial on the issue. Attorneys can negotiate a reasonable settlement based on an understanding of the details of the case and the history of outcomes of litigation related to similar cases in the particular county.

One can make a reasonable guess as to the outcome of a trial; but one cannot guarantee the outcome of any trial, because a jury involves so many individuals and their own perceptions of an issue. Even Aristotle labelled rhetoric as an art rather than a science. If something is considered a science one can predict a specific outcome of a combination of materials related to that something; science is consistent, objective, and rational. Two plus two equals four; always and in any condition. If something is an art, one understands that the perception of that something may differ across individuals—as the idiom states, "beauty is in the eye of the beholder." As another idiom states, "one man's trash is another man's treasure."

Rhetoric may be considered an art, but it is influenced by science. While pointing to rhetoric as an art, Aristotle made the connection between rhetoric and biology (Aristotle, translated 1991). A growing body of scholarship in cognitive neuroscience is helping politicians, marketers, and attorneys understand why certain messages and how they are presented affect an audience a certain way. All attempt to use a combination of stimuli to affect an audience's perception of a message; that is why it is important to consider neuroscientific attributes that are involved in multimodal persuasive messages, which is the goal of this book.

Theories about multimodal composition continue to thrive as technology changes provide more access to various modes of representation for audiences and improved quality. Video is now integrated within websites effortlessly, and improving Internet access speeds make viewing video less arduous than before. While advertisers have been placing video commercials online for some time, many companies are now placing video reports and other multimodal messages online. Simons and Jones (2011) allude to some attributes of a persuasive message that may be multimodal in nature, referring to neural processes involved. Specifically, they consider the roles images can play in affecting an audience's perception of an object or person, and they encourage integrating the full range of resources and tools humans have to communicate (p. 124).

This book attempts to make the connections between these rhetorical choices and a growing understanding of neuroscience explicit by linking the different disciplinary fields using concepts familiar to both but that are not explicitly stated in the literature. As I indicated in *How the Brain Processes Multimodal Technical Instructions* (*HTB*), I do this for two reasons: 1) in an effort to help students and professionals understand these connections better toward encouraging faculty and practitioners across various disciplines, including business, communication, and law, to implement this information to help facilitate learning and application of persuasive rhetoric, especially within multimodal settings such as commercials, videos, oral presentations, and even business or technical proposals that integrate graphics; and 2) to link rhetoric further within the growing STEM education tradition that seems to emphasize science and math education over humanities, thereby showing the relevance of rhetoric in this educational approach as I did in that previous book (Remley, 2015).

In this chapter, I provide an overview of the literature in neuroscience, which I will integrate throughout the book. I also introduce connections between rhetoric and neuroscience, laying a foundation on which to build a model of persuasive rhetoric that integrates elements of neuroscience. Some of this is a review from *HTB*, but I link it to persuasive rhetoric instead of instruction and learning.

Theoretical Bases

Neurobiologists Calvert, Spence, and Stein (2004) note that, because the scholarship related to neuroscience is "spread across multiple disciplines, it has become increasingly fragmented in recent years" (p. xii). However, in a special issue of *Technical Communication Quarterly*, Rivers (2011) encourages a multidisciplinary approach to research into cognitive science, recognizing the roles that biology and social environment as well as technology play in cognition. Alluding to the convergence of tools, environment, and brain in distributed cognition, he states that, "those tools and that world are always part of the mind itself" (p. 415).

The field of social semiotics, further, recognizes that meaning is a social construct; that is, one's interpretation of various images and objects evolves through interactions with others. The cognitive experience is rhetorical and social. As I detailed in a previous book, we learn about new concepts by interacting with phenomena associated with the new concepts; however, it also applies to persuasion. One may provide information to us in a way that will help us to understand a new concept or convince us to take a different position than one we originally hold; this is both a social phenomenon—interaction with another, and it is rhetorical—a message is provided to an audience (us) with a particular purpose. It takes interaction with the world around us to comprehend a situation and the meaning of the information provided. However, even Aristotle noted a biological attribute to rhetoric. Cognitive science, generally, recognizes these attributes of cognition—social and biological attributes related to facilitating an understanding of our world. However, the discussion of these cognitive neuroscience dynamics is complicated by disciplinary discourses and exclusions.

I called attention previously to the fact that each discipline approaches the topic from its own angle, recognizing that literature from that field is needed to support such scholarship (2015). For example, rarely will the author of a scholarly article cite work from outside their own discipline or the discipline of the particular journal. This extends to scholarly books, too. For example, in his highly regarded book *Cognition in the Wild*, Hutchins (1996) limits the discussion of cognition and social semiotics to cognitive psychology and distributed knowledge theory. Also, in *How the Mind Works*, another highly regarded work of cognitive neuroscience, Pinker (1997) integrates some discussion of neuroscience on cognitive processes; however, he focuses on historical development of cognitive processes and psychological evolution. Finally, Gruber (2012) highlights discourse differences in how scholars treat the neuro-scientific concept of mirror neurons, neurons that help an audience interpret and copy behavior they view. Such discourse exclusion limits the lens through which studies examine the phenomena. However, the phenomenon itself is very much a part of the principles of social discourse and persuasive rhetoric; one must use an audience's expectations and values to make an argument or persuade, and using discourse from one's own field helps to make a particularly scholarly case because the audience expects it and values it accordingly.

Rhetoric, in a broad sense, examines how the way information is presented affects an audience's understanding of that information and response to it. Aristotle (translated 1991) and Perelman and Olbrechts-Tyteca (1969) recognized that rhetoric considers the disposition of certain kinds of audiences and one who wishes to convey an effective message must adjust to their particular audience. Aristotle acknowledges that rhetoric includes "three factors—the speaker, the subject and the listener—and it is to the last of these that its purpose it intended" (p. 80). The purpose of a message and its audience are intertwined. The message must consider the audience's disposition in order to accomplish its purpose. This disposition can be theorized relative to social disposition or biological/physical disposition. Indeed, Aristotle notes that this likely involves an audience that may have "limited intellectual scope and limited capacity to follow an extended chain of reasoning" (p. 76). Such a statement includes physiological attributes in the rhetoric equation. If the audience's cognitive capacities are not considered in developing the message, the meaning of the message will be lost.

Perelman and Olbrechts-Tyteca recall this emphasis on the audience, pointing out that "it is in terms of an audience that an argumentation develops" (p. 5). Indeed, they compare one who does not consider the audience to a rude visitor (p. 17). They assert that the most important rule of rhetoric is to adapt the message to the audience (p. 25). A message is not automatically understood just because it is articulated; it must be conveyed in a way that suits the audience's background and understandings, their experiences and practices; their capacity for cognition.

Scholarship in rhetoric draws on studies from the social science and humanities disciplines of cognitive neuroscience—social semiotics, social psychology, and language theories. Rhetoric is certainly a social dynamic. However, rhetoric has been left out of much of the discussion of cognitive neuroscience and is not considered amongst those fields.

Jack (2012) provides some introductory material for connecting rhetoric with biological fields of neuroscience in her edited collection about "neurorhetorics." Jack and Appelbaum (2010) identify two approaches to "neurorhetoric." One involves studying the rhetoric of neuroscience, in which one considers how different discourses treat neuroscientific scholarship. Gruber (2012), for example, takes the first approach and describes the discourse differences related to how different fields treat a particular concept of neuroscience—the concept of "mirror neurons." He observes that institutional dynamics at work within disciplinary scholarship limit the ability to arrive at a common language to describe the concept, further illustrating this problem. Jack and Applebaum (2010) also state that,

> [a] second approach might be the neuroscience of rhetoric, drawing new insights into language, persuasion, and communication from neuroscience research. Findings such as this study of noncommunicative patients can prompt us to broaden our very definitions of rhetoric to include those with impaired communication (such as autism, aphasia, or "locked-in syndrome"), asking how communication occurs through different means, or how brain differences might influence communication. (p. 10)

I attempt to close some of the discourse disconnections Gruber (2012) and Calvert, Spence, and Stein (2004) identify while using the second approach to synthesize scholarship in multimodal rhetoric and neurobiology, particularly with respect to multisensory neural processes, explicitly in the discussion of cognitive neuroscience.

Gruber formulates four "Pillars" by which interdisciplinary research involving rhetoric and neuroscience can occur by facilitating a means of "translation" between discourses. These pillars are very much a building tool applied in this book. The first pillar, he explains, is the "field-familiar spokesperson" (p. 237). This is a scholar who is knowledgeable about neuroscience and a second field—a sort of intermediary between discourses. I represent this person in the context of this book. The second pillar is that of the spokesperson's support—a mechanism by which the spokesperson from Pillar 1 establishes ethos, or credibility, as well as logos for establishing the connection with the neuroscience community (p. 239). As I explained in the Author's Preface of *HTB*, I consulted with a neurobiologist to ascertain that I understood concepts of neurobiology that I presented and applied them correctly. This neurobiologist acts as the second pillar in the context of this book.

The third pillar is that of nature; Gruber indicates that nature connects neuroscience with the particular field being applied to it or vice-versa. I have already alluded to Aristotle's and Perleman and Olbrechts-Tyteca's references to the links between rhetoric and biology. These and the scholarship in neurobiology that I cite contribute to establishing this pillar for this book. The last pillar Gruber identifies is that of "objective writing practice." He explains that this is a practice that makes writing transparent rather than an exercise in creativity; it is an effort to represent an objective reality rather than corrupt reality. Persuasion pertains to an audience's perception of reality, which is based heavily on the audience's prior experiences; consequently, I use that conception of objective reality within the model.

The model that I proposed and develop here further rests on these pillars and is open to further construction. As scholars in rhetoric and other disciplines interact with this model, they act as additional field-familiar spokespersons, lending their credibility to the model's development and applications. When two or more researchers from different fields join to study a given phenomenon, a synergistic effect occurs within the dynamic of those pillars to strengthen the model and allow for further development.

Cognitive Neuroscience and Rhetoric

The field of neuroscience has experienced a boom in scholarship that integrates several disciplines. Generally, this scholarship ranges across the five general disciplines that are connected with cognitive neuroscience: cognitive psychology, philosophy, linguistics, biology, and chemistry. Physics is also somewhat involved. Most of these are recognized as "humanities"-related areas, while the others are specifically connected to "science"—biology, chemistry, and physics. As mentioned above, each discipline theorizes neuroscience and cognition by applying its own research methods and theories to analysis and discussion. However, the disconnection across disciplines is problematic, especially as institutions attempt to find ways to connect disciplines with inter-disciplinary programs and research projects. Cognition is associated closely with perception; how one perceives information affects their understanding of that information. The field of cognitive neuroscience devotes much attention to understanding how one processes information toward cognition.

Humanities scholars tend to examine how language and social interactions affect our understanding of the world. Reid (2007) notes that "cognitive scientists termed the 1990s 'the Decade of the Brain' for the startling advances made throughout their discipline" (p. 14). Indeed,

Hutchins (1996) and Pinker (1997) theorize cognition as a series of developmental processes that include historical dynamics as well as how people treat training and actual practice and social dynamics thereof. This has helped to generate subfields of distributed cognition and cognitive psychology as well as social semiotics. In each case, research in cognitive neuroscience has found that cognition is a multisensory process. Social interaction engages multiple senses—visual, aural, spatial orientation, and relationship, as well as gesture, touch, and smell. Likewise, language is generally recognized as being aural/oral or visual—print-linguistic text is a visual representation.

Science disciplines have been studying connections between perception, behavior, and neural dynamics. Available technology affects how this study occurs. Until recently most of this involved looking at electrical activity within the brain. Neurons send electrical messages across the brain, and the different parts process that information toward doing something with it. However, recent technology has made it possible to look into other physical attributes of the brain and how the brain processes information related to perception and cognition. In particular, two-photon microscopes and magnetic resonance imaging (MRI) technology facilitates such research. Two-photon microscopes permit the imaging of areas of the brain that are excited during tasks, suggesting neural activity. Some MRI technology allows researchers to see how blood flows to certain parts of the brain while one performs a particular task—viewing a given film or doing certain work. This technology is called "functional MRI," or "fMRI." Biologists and chemists have begun examining the relationship between blood flow and neural processes. As humanities scholarship has done, many of these studies also link cognition to multi-sensory processes (for example, see collections edited by Calvert, Spence, and Stein, 2004; and Murray and Wallace, 2012).

Rhetoric encompasses a range of communication practices including informational messages, persuasive messages, and instructional messages. I focused on instructional messages in a previous book; my focus in the book is on the neuro-rhetoric of persuasion. Some studies have found that persuasion involves some different neural activities than cognition related to cognition does (Azar, 2010; Pillay, 2011; and Ramsay et al., 2013). There is more self-reflection and reflection about one's perception of others and attitudes. Persuasion is a belief-oriented or attitude-oriented concept. The general focus of persuasion is to change one's attitude or beliefs about a given topic or issue or to elicit a stronger conviction in belief or attitude about that topic or issue. While mirror neurons, for example, are involved in this process as well, that involvement has more to do with mirroring or sharing a perception ("shared emotion") than with copying or imitating action. Pillay points out that "...our brains can mirror not only actions, but intentions as well" (p. 63). When a manager or supervisor seems to treat a situation as negative, subordinates seem to perceive it similarly, as their brain mirrors the supervisor's perception of the situation.

Persuasive Rhetoric

I introduce some concepts of persuasion in this section, because they provide much of the basic rhetoric-related components to theorizing multi-modal persuasion and neuroscience. Aristotle laid the primary foundation of persuasion, and Perelman and Olbrechts-Tyteca modified that foundation to account for less scientific aspects of reasoning. Their theories are most prominent for the sake of this book, and I refer to them several times in different chapters.

A basic premise of persuasion is that the audience is in a position to be moved to change their perception of a given issue such that a reasonable persuasive message could effect that change. For example, if one is not in the market to buy a new car—because they just purchased one, they are very happy with their current vehicle or cannot afford to buy a new car, even the most persuasive car commercial will have no effect on that viewer. One need not explicitly be in the market for a new car, but one should be willing to consider such a purchase in order for the commercial to have any meaningful effect.

Another basic component of persuasion is the variety of ways an audience can be moved: these are generally recognized as logos (reason/logic), ethos (speaker's/writer's credibility), and pathos (appeal to emotion). Most scholarship in rhetoric finds that a combination of approaches works best such that a message may combine speaker's credibility with logic (ethos and logos). An example is when a physician states that many studies find a link between smoking and cancer such that it is reasonable to conclude that smoking can cause cancer; the audience understands the physician to be expertly trained in how the body reacts to various chemicals and trusts that the physician is speaking the truth (ethos). Further, because many studies find that link, it is reasonable to make the conclusion about cause (smoking) and effect (cancer)—(logos). These approaches are important to this book because of the many ways the approaches can be used in a multimodal message. One's perception of a speaker/writer can be affected by the various ways used to deliver the message, whether in person or via some technological medium. Likewise, logos and pathos can mix to create an effective, moving persuasive message. If an audience feels some connection with the speaker, there is a certain bond that may disarm an audience or make it less resistant.

A particular phenomenon associated with persuasion conveyed by Perelman and Olbrechts-Tyteca (1969) is that of a quasi-logical argument. They argued that perception is subjective rather than objective. Different audiences have a different understanding of the world based on each's experiences. One who has grown up in a wealthy environment is not likely to understand the hunger one who has grown up in poverty may have faced on a regular basis. As such, one audience may perceive an argument to be very logical/reasonable while another may not because of each audience's relative experiences and understanding of the world. So, a persuasive message may work well with one audience but not with another audience. A speaker/writer needs to consider aspects of the audience's relationship to the situation as he or she designs a message that will engage the particular audience most effectively.

I elaborate on these in another chapter. However, the basic purpose of persuasion is to change an audience's perception of something toward a new perception.

Multimodality

The field of multimodal rhetoric, especially, considers how various modes of representation affect an audience's ability to make meaning about the information provided with those combinations. Rhetoric is already linked implicitly to the social sciences disciplines of cognitive neuroscience through existing scholarship related to social semiotics and cognition (e.g.: Gee, 2003; Hutchins, 1995; Kress, 2003; Moreno and Mayer, 2000; New London Group, 1996; and Tufte, 2003). I connect scholarship of multimodal rhetoric explicitly to the scientific fields of cognitive neuroscience relative to cognition associated with persuasion in this book. Also, I argue that scholarship in rhetoric can inform studies related to other areas of cognitive neuroscience. The fields are already somewhat connected by terminology that can act as a bridge to facilitate interdisciplinary research.

Neurobiologists refer to neural processes that integrate multiple senses as "multisensory integration." The term "multisensory integration" is the biological equivalent of the term "multimodal" in rhetoric. In fact, neurobiologists sometimes refer to "multisensory integration" as "multimodal integration." While "multimodal" in rhetoric pertains to multiple modes of representation used to convey a message, "multisensory integration" refers to the interaction of multiple senses used at the same time to process information. As Sheridan, Ridolfo, and Michel (2012) noted, "[h]umans experience the world through multiple senses simultaneously...A speech delivered in a public forum is a complex performance that involves not just words, but gestures, facial expressions, intonation and more..." (p. xiv). Our brain processes these different forms of representation—aural, visual, spatial—toward cognition.

In neuroscience the modes of representation are treated as "stimuli" from which neurons initiate information processing. So, a visual representation—a photograph, for example—would stimulate neurons associated with visual information processing. Likewise, a message that included visual and audio forms of representation, like a commercial that includes video and audio narration or a speech, would be considered a form of multimodal rhetoric from a rhetoric perspective, and it involves multimodal integration from a neurobiological perspective. This link is natural and logical for two other reasons.

Rhetoric and Science

Rhetoric is already linked and theorized relative to the humanities and social sciences. While this link will continue to be pursued, and should be pursued, it is important to recognize biological attributes that affect rhetoric. As Reid (2007) observes, "all information, even speech, enters our body in analog form" through various sensory experiences (p. 17). Neurons help to process it toward facilitating meaning-making and cognition of the information. However, rarely are biological attributes of cognition factored into the discussion of rhetoric. Scholarship in rhetoric tends to focus on the product and its effect, not the process that affects that effect. Studies of brain disorders and how such disorders or injuries affect learning and perception are occurring. An understanding of the processes in the brain can contribute to designing more effective messages.

So, one reason to encourage a closer connection between rhetoric and science is to recognize that biological dynamic that affects how an audience responds to a message. Leaving biology out of rhetoric is like a writing teacher grading an essay based only on the product and not caring about the writing process. Any writing teacher recognizes that practice as bad pedagogy. It is generally recognized in writing studies that if a writing teacher understands the process by which the student composed the essay, he or she can provide much better instruction to help improve the student's writing process toward improving their writing than by focusing only on a writing product and identifying errors.

As I mentioned above, a second reason for my theorization relative to science is political in nature, recognizing the current academic environment. Academic programs associated with science, technology, engineering, and math (STEM disciplines) are receiving higher consideration for funding and marketing. Social science and humanities disciplines have to defend their relevance in the current environment, and many are facing reduced funding. It is important to show the relevance of rhetoric to this STEM-fever so that interdisciplinary research that recognizes the value of rhetoric can occur. However, this relevance is not superficial; it is very much credible and valid. Rhetoric can make an impact in science-oriented programs. A text making this connection, introducing a discourse that integrates language from both fields and talking about contributions of such research and their impact can introduce such interdisciplinary scholarship.

I theorize multimodal rhetoric pertaining to persuasion by weaving neuro-scientific theory, particularly referring to neurobiological studies associated with electrophysiology (patterns of electrical flow within the brain) and hemodynamic attributes of brain processes (studies of blood flow to certain parts of the brain associated with sensory experiences and cognition), with multimodal theory. Using existing theories of multimodal rhetoric and studies related to electrophysiology and the hemo-neural hypothesis, I develop a discourse model that integrates elements from both fields uniting them. This theorization is easily facilitated because much of what scholarship in multimodal rhetoric has found is re-enforced in scholarship connected to neural processes. Indeed, neural process studies help to explain some of the biological attributes connected to findings of multimodal scholarship; that is, it helps us understand *why*, from a biological perspective, certain multimodal products facilitate a better understanding of information than other multimodal products.

Through synthesizing multimodal rhetorical theory with what is understood about how the mind processes information related to learning tasks and concepts relative to its use of blood, it is possible to refine that theory as it pertains specifically to training/instruction and process improvement, two topics of considerable interest in both industry and education. I review extant theories of multimodality and neuroscience—particularly related to two methods associated with bio-physiological analysis—electrophysiology and the hemo-neural hypothesis. Throughout the book I also discuss workplace and educational applications of the model relative to persuasive rhetoric, particularly cases that pertain to marketing, political science, and legal studies. I use different approaches in different chapters to show various ways the model can be applied to an analysis or considerations associated with developing a persuasive message.

With each of these applications, I discuss the inter-relationships of the various modes of representation associated with cognition. It is necessary to integrate neurobiological terminology to explain why certain multimodal combinations and rhetoric works. I review some of this literature in the remainder of this chapter. I avoid thick description of these studies, and I provide definitions of several terms in order to provide a primer for interdisciplinary theorization. For example, while I describe relevant concepts such as "mirror neurons" (to which I alluded much earlier in this chapter), I do not refer to specialized names given to neuron types such as "F5 neurons." One does not need to be a biologist to understand findings related to bio-neurological and neurobiological studies and their connection with multimodal rhetoric; however, one needs to be able to understand and use some terms in order to appreciate the discourse of the discipline from which the analysis comes.

In this overview, I also identify specific theories of neurobiology that I use in my own theorization connecting these disciplines. Four specific concepts connected to neurobiology are involved with this effort: 1) multimodality of neurons; 2) "reward neurons;" 3) "mirror neurons;" and 4) neural plasticity. Further, this theorization integrates neurobiological perspectives of multimodal rhetoric, including the Colavita visual dominance effect. Rhetoric scholars recognize the role visual rhetoric plays and it has been theorized considerably; however, none of it has integrated the notion of the Colavita visual dominance effect. In addition to their interest in dynamics related to visual information, neuro-physiologists also recognize the important role of previous experience and knowledge in cognition as well as how information is presented relative to modes involved and timing of presentation, similar to the findings associated with Moreno and Mayer (2000). These are integrated into the model that I present. However, I provide some details of the three neurobiological theories that serve as the foundation of the biological attributes of the discussion next. This information repeats a section from Chapter 1 of a previous book.

Neural Research Methods

Data collection facilitates careful analysis toward theorization. The means by which data collection is facilitated play a very important role in the nature of the data used. Neurophysiologists and neurobiologists tend to use three different methods that involve different technologies. Sometimes these studies will integrate more than one approach in an effort to triangulate data. I describe these three approaches here to provide an understanding of how data is collected within the field of neurobiology.

Electrophysiology

A popular approach to study neural activity is through studying electrical waves sent across the brain as one performs a particular task. Electrodes are placed on various parts of the head, and they monitor signals suggesting certain neural activity. Such technology is affected by the tool's capacity to measure multiple neurons and its range covering the area of the brain. Older technology was limited to studying very few neurons and electrodes were most sensitive to activity near where they were placed. So, they could not monitor much activity.

More recently, technology enables researchers to study more neurons and a larger area of the brain. Consequently, it is now possible to have a better understanding of what is happening with various neurons as one performs a task. However, it is still uncertain as to what activity is specifically occurring at cell-level.

Two-Photon Microscopes

As indicated above, powerful microscopes are able to provide an image of the brain as one performs a given task. Two-photon microscopes allow researchers to view activity; however, this is generally limited to study of smaller animals given the size of the microscope and radiation. However, it is possible to theorize human neurobiology from certain small animals such as rats. A constraint of the 2-photon microscope, though, is that it is limited to studying tissue closer to the brain surface than most neural activity occurs.

Hemo-Neural Hypothesis

It is generally held that neurons in the brain facilitate many cognitive processes. Neurons help to transport information from one part of the brain, as it is acquired, to other parts of the brain, where it may be processed. It is generally recognized that this is an electrical process, making electrophysiology a valid approach to studying the brain processes; this is what forms the foundation of computational theories of the mind. The brain is like a computer. Several studies note the relationship between neural disorders and cognition.

Also, the brain includes a vast system of vessels carrying blood to various parts of the brain. Indeed, as Gross (1998) points out, Aristotle believed the manifestation of the activity of this system of veins to be emotion, intelligence, and action (p. 247). Moore and Cao (2008) note that blood flow in the brain "is typically well correlated with neural activity" (p. 2035). As such, they surmise that blood-flow can be an indicator of neural activity, citing several attributes of computational theory and intelligence derived from the Turing Test (Turing, 1950). Moore and Cao (2008, p. 2041) state that,

> In many cognitive paradigms, blood flow modulation occurs in anticipation of or independent of the receipt of sensory input. One example of a context in which hemo-neural modulation of cortical dynamics may impact information processing is through enhancement of evoked responses during selective attention. A wide variety of studies has shown that attention to a region of input space (e.g., a retinotopic position or body area) is correlated with enhanced evoked action potential firing of cortical neurons with receptive fields overlapping the attended region (Bichot and Desimone, 2006). These effects typically emerge 100–500 ms after the onset of attentional focus (Khayat et al., 2006; Khoe et al., 2006; Worden et al., 2000). (p. 2041)

In short, they theorize that the connection between neural activity and blood flow is so closely correlated that the two suggest a relationship by which neural activity can be measured by blood flow to certain parts of the brain relative to performance of particular tasks. For example, in highly visual task-oriented studies, a larger amount of blood is observed to flow to the visual (or occipital) cortex than otherwise observed. As such, it is possible to use blood flow—hemodynamics—to study neural activity and cognitive processes. Blood flow can facilitate analysis of neural inhibition (neurons being subdued or prevented from activity) and neural excitation (neural activity increasing). They indicate that fMRI technology allows researchers to observe and measure blood flow and, thus, to infer neurological processes *in vivo*, important to ascertaining such correlation and analysis (Cao, 2011).

Such findings of correlation between neural activity and blood flow suggest that multiple biological systems are at work within cognition. Much as multimodal rhetoric research has discovered that presenting information using multiple modes may affect cognition better than providing it within a single mode, multiple systems within the brain may be involved in processing information or facilitating such information processing. Rather than one system doing all the work, multiple systems contribute to cognitive processes.

Several studies use this hemo-neural hypothesis to theorize neural processes related to cognition and others use it to triangulate data from EEG methods (see collections edited by Calvert, Spence, and Stein, 2004; and Murray and Wallace, 2012). Further, these studies assert conclusions consistent with studies of multimodal rhetoric, explaining some of the biology behind those conclusions.

The topic of technology has been part of rhetoric and composition scholarship for several years now. Integrating neurobiological studies into the study of the rhetoric of technology opens the door to further analyses of how technologies influence research and contribute to new knowledge about cognitive processes and ways to present information productively to facilitate cognition. Neurobiologists, for example, have studied the ways that simulators affect neural processes, examining blood flow across the brain as subjects interacted with a simulator. Multimodal rhetoric scholars have studied the use of simulators in learning by having subjects perform certain tasks after interacting with a simulator; however, they do not integrate a discussion of neural processes involved in that interaction. Combining research methods and analyses from both fields into a single study may enhance such studies.

Multimodality of Neurons

There are two kinds of neurons identified in the neurobiological literature relative to modal attributes: uni-modal and multi-modal. Uni-modal neurons carry information relative to a single modality. For example, a uni-modal auditory neuron can process only auditory information. Multimodal neurons are neurons that can carry information relative to more than one mode. A multimodal neuron may be able to process information from both visual and auditory senses (multimodal). A neuron that can carry information relative to three different modes is particularly labeled as tri-modal; however, it can be discussed within the multimodal neuron category.

Again, older technologies tended to focus on uni-modal neuron activity because of their limited capacity; but more recent technology is able to show multi-modality of neurons. There is no debate about the existence of these modal characteristics; however, there is some debate regarding whether particular sets of neurons act independently of one another and can manage facilitating individual sensory information and then bring it together computationally, or if they can facilitate multiple sensory information (Allman, Keniston, and Meredith, 2009; Allman and Meredith, 2007; and Bernstein, Auer, and Moore, 2004).

Studies related to multimodal neurons also suggest that certain kinds of information can be processed at different rates by such neurons, suggesting an optimal modal composition of a given message to facilitate faster processing (Bethge, Rotermund, and Pawelzik, 2003; and Bremner and Spence, 2008). Numerous studies in multimodal rhetoric examine combinations that have the best effect on an audience (Kress, 2011; and Moreno and Mayer, 2000). Studies in assessment of multimodal products contribute to this analysis as well (Ball, 2003; Katz and Odell, 2012; Neal, 2011; and Remley, 2012). As such, multimodal rhetoric scholars can contribute to studies related to ascertaining optimal combinations by developing potential multimodal products that can be used in empirical electrophysiological or fMRI studies.

Reward Neurons

Several studies related to dopamine, a neuro-transmitter, recognize that the stimulated neurons are associated with perception of rewards and motivation. Activation of these neurons helps to enhance attention by conveying some kind of motivation to behave a certain way to the audience affected. Advertisers integrate sex often into commercials, because it has shown to activate reward neurons. People pay closer attention when those neurons are activated. Reward neurons play into persuasive messages when a speaker acknowledges some benefit the audience may experience.

There are many ways a reward may be experienced, further. For example, I may receive some financial benefit—a bonus; or I may feel that I am even more a part of a certain social group; or I may feel good about helping someone else. All of these act to motivate me to act a certain way because I perceive I will be rewarded somehow.

Mirror Neurons

Gallese et al. (2007) and Rizzolatti et al. (1996) first reported on the existence of neurons that appear to facilitate cognition of movements and behaviors that one observes another perform while doing a given task. Even before the observer tries to perform the same task he or she observed, he or she has acquired a sense of how to perform the task through a mental visual mirror. Further, they observe a connection between these neurobiological phenomena and social science. Gallese et al. state,

> Suppose one sees someone else grasping a cup. Mirror neurons for grasping will most likely be activated in the observer's brain. The direct matching between the observed action and its motor representation in the observer's brain, however, can tell us only what the action is (it's a grasp) and not why the action occurred. (p. 135)

Mirror neurons facilitate much of the cognition associated with experiential learning and hands-on training. However, they also contribute to persuasion in that an audience wants to mirror some aspect of the speaker or the speaker may want to resemble some aspect of the audience as a way to assimilate with it more. In this way, they act differently in persuasive exchanges than they do in instructional exchanges. In a persuasive message, they help facilitate a shared experience between speaker and audience (Pillay, 2011).

Neural Plasticity

In cognitive neuroscience, plasticity pertains to the ability of neurons to change their composition and behaviors relative to the information they process and the person's experiences. As we interact with the world our neurons change to help us understand how to respond to various situations we encounter. Two parts of the brain closely connected to plasticity are the amygdala and the hippocampus. I describe more about these a bit later in this section.

Neurobiologists recognize, much as humanities scholars such as Gee, Pinker, and Mayer, that experience plays a role in learning about information and values. What one understands of a given bit of information and how they tend to best learn information affects how they learn new information. Berlucchi and Buchtel (2009) define neural plasticity as:

> changes in neural organization which may account for various forms of behavioral modifiability, either short-lasting or enduring, including maturation, adaptation to a mutable environment, specific and unspecific kinds of learning, and compensatory adjustments in response to functional losses from aging or brain damage. (p. 307)

Studies related to plasticity tend to examine how one responds to a series of subsequent experiences of certain modal combinations after first exposure, especially related to cognitive development. Generally, the brain is able to process information more quickly as it learns more about that information. Depending on the amount of exposure to information and the way the information is provided, cognition about the information can occur more quickly.

Because plasticity is affected by social interaction over time, culture also impacts persuasive rhetoric; a particular message may have a better persuasive effect in one culture but not another merely because of social expectations and perceptions of rewards or attributes of the product itself. There is a special connection between culture and persuasion because of how our brain responds to cultural influences, but some of our responses are simply natural.

The hippocampus is a place in the brain that helps us store information about our experiences. How was the experience? How did we react? Was our reaction appropriate and did we benefit from our reaction? If not, how can we change our reaction so when we experience it again we know to respond that same way? This is culturally determined through social interactions. As a young child, when I respond to a new event or experience and receive positive feedback from my parents or others whose feedback I value, I learn that my response was appropriate. Over time, then, I learn to respond that way in similar situations.

Likewise, our basic desire for self-preservation impacts our responses to people or events that we do not understand or that we did not like; such people and events invoke fear in us, persuading us against doing them in the future. The amygdala is part of the neurological system in the brain that concerns these basic desires. We are born with the desire to stay alive, and the amygdala helps us do that by sending signals to the brain when we encounter something new that may be dangerous to us. Young children—less than 4 years old, for example—often cry when a stranger speaks to them, and they clutch a parent's leg or torso. This is a reaction to the fear of this new experience. The child does not know who the new person is and responds with fear, grabbing what it knows will protect it. Plasticity is part of this dynamic because we experience events that affected us negatively, and we try to avoid them in the future. Over time, our neurons have associated that event or person with fear.

Another area of plasticity study is the effect of brain injuries or disorders on cognition. Some scholarship in rhetoric theorizes relative to such disorders and injuries. For example, there is some study in the fields of rhetoric and cognitive psychology about how to facilitate learning among those with autism. However, less study in how such disorders affect persuasion exists.

Because of this body of literature that overlaps much of what has been done in multimodal rhetoric scholarship and the growing interest in interdisciplinary study, it is important for disciplines to find ways to synthesize their work. The disciplinary divide related to discourse differences discourages such interdisciplinarity, and scholars in both areas recognize how this negatively impacts the study of cognition. However, this text attempts to build a bridge by which rhetoric and social science scholars can contribute to biomedical cognitive neuroscientists; and, consequently recognize the value of rhetoric scholarship in STEM programs and vice versa. I outline the remainder of the book in the following section.

Overview of Book

In the second chapter, I review extant literature that I have mentioned in this chapter to detail connections between the science-oriented fields of cognitive neuroscience and multimodal rhetoric. I connect multimodal rhetoric theory with perspectives about multisensory processing from neurobiology. This review also facilitates identification of some attributes of multimodality that contribute to an integrated theory of multimodality; this theory integrates elements of bio-physiology and rhetoric.

In Chapters 3 and 4, I detail the theoretical model; and I provide analyses of cases related to it in a handful of subsequent chapters. Such analyses provide illustrations of possible ways to apply the new model to analyze multimodal rhetoric and neuroscience via an interdisciplinary approach. In one chapter I demonstrate use of the model toward producing multimodal persuasive messages. Finally, I suggest implications of using the new model in practice, suggesting further research as well as providing a rubric to facilitate production and assessment in instructional and practical applications.

I do not provide many images to show the reader particular attributes or items. I made an effort to acquire permission to use some images; however, in my experience, I found that many copyright holders of such images would like to have some control over how their images are used and discussed. In an effort to compensate for the lack of images, I try to provide a detailed description of the content of the image to help the reader visualize it. I, also, include enough information in the list of references to help the reader access many of the particular images directly.

2 Multimodality and Neurobiology

One of the goals of this book is to raise awareness that neural activity affects how different modal combinations may work best for certain purposes and certain audiences or individuals. Studies like Moreno and Mayer's (2000) brought attention to the issue of optimal modal combinations for learning, but we do not know why those combinations worked well in that particular set of experiments. Neuroscience is the study of how neurons in various parts of the brain act under various stimuli. Cognitive neuroscience focuses study on these actions relative to learning. That is, it considers how the brain responds to various stimuli when the brain is tasked with a learning activity. However, some of this scholarship also applies to persuasion. The field of cognitive neuroscience integrates several fields including cognitive psychology, philosophy, chemistry, and biology. Much of what I cover in this chapter is also provided in *HTB* (Remley, 2015); however, I link it more to the focus of this book on persuasive rhetoric.

In this chapter, I review scholarship related to cognitive neuroscience and its multisensory attributes. I eliminate biological jargon to focus attention on the general link between the fields of neuroscience and multimodal rhetoric. This information sheds light on the effects certain messages have on people when multiple modes are used to present information. Limiting the terminology to a small set of new vocabulary will also help transition rhetoricians to the science-oriented language.

Little scholarship in multimodal rhetoric uses the scholarship from the field of cognitive neuroscience. One reason for this is that the biology associated with neuroscience quickly becomes complex for most people to understand. It includes thick discussions of neurons and how information travels around the brain, integrating very specialized language associated with the biology of the brain. I try to describe some related scientific concepts without using that jargon.

The scientific fields—physics, chemistry, and biology, and related subfields—tend to focus study on neuron behaviors. Neurons are often considered as a network of information processing paths. Summarizing this network: neurons have three principle parts: the cell body; axons, which carry information away from the cell body; and dendrites, which carry information to the cell body. The junction between two neurons is called the synapse. Dendrites take sensory information in, and axons send information out. The neural process involves a signal being sent from the axon of one neuron to the dendrite of another neuron via synapses. However, the brain develops new neurons in developmental stages of life, and other neurons die as we mature and grow old.

Analysis of hemodynamics (via fMRI) and electrophysiology (via EEG) pertaining to neurons helps researchers understand which parts of the brain are working most during certain kinds of activities. Different cortices are associated with different functions. As more blood moves to a given cortex of the brain, the implication is that the particular neural functions of that cortex are more actively engaged than are other parts of the brain; this is referred to as the "hemo-neural hypothesis" (Moore and Cao, 2008). Tools such as fMRI help identify patterns of neural activity and blood flow. Most of the research prior to 2000 focused on particular, individual modal dynamics; how the brain operates when stimulated by a single particular mode—e.g.: hearing, vision, or touch. However, advances in MRI technology allow closer examinations, and recent studies have found that more than one sense is generally engaged in various activities, but to varying degrees based on the activity.

There is considerable literature in the neurobiological field of cognitive neuroscience that characterizes learning as a multisensory experience (see collections edited by Calvert, Spence, and Stein, 2004; and Murray and Wallace, 2012). I reviewed and summarized several of these relative to instructional materials in *HTB* (Remley, 2015). Work in neuro-marketing, also, connects neurobiology with rhetoric relative to persuasion (see, for example, Dooley, 2012; and Nahai, 2012).

Smell is also included in the sensory experience; for example, according to Gass and Seiter (2014), "Ambient fragrances can enhance mood, improve task performance and influence consumer behavior" (p. 349). Krishna, Elder, and Caldara (2010) link touch and smell to consumer behaviors, indicating that smell plays a role in purchasing behavior.

Multimodal Integration and Cognition

As I mentioned in Chapter 1, recognizing that multiple senses are involved in cognition, neurobiologists refer to multisensory processes as "multisensory integration," or "multimodal integration." This terminology helps facilitate a connection with multimodal rhetoric. However, I want, first, to review very generally how multimodality is treated in the field of rhetoric. This sets up a more detailed discussion of that literature and connections with neurobiology.

Many recent studies of literate practices have discussed multimodality more explicitly (Gee, 2003; Lemke, 1998 and 1999; Mayer, 2005; Moreno and Mayer, 2000; the New London Group, 1996; Richards,

2003; and Whithaus, 2012). The New London Group, which is comprised of several literacy scholars, identify five different, unique modes of representation: print-linguistic, visual, audio, gestural, spatial; and they acknowledge that any two or more of these can be combined to form a multimodal representation. They acknowledge that,

> we argue that literacy pedagogy now must account for the burgeoning variety of text forms associated with information and multimedia technologies. This includes understanding and competent control of representational forms that are becoming increasingly significant in the overall communications environment, such as visual images and their relationship to the written word-for instance, visual design in desktop publishing or the interface of visual and linguistic meaning in multimedia. (p. 60)

Since the New London Group published this article, researchers have been considering various combinations of modes of representation that can affect meaning-making. Further, scholars realize that pedagogy needs to integrate instruction in composing with these different modes of representation. The importance of graphic images in these literate practices is noteworthy because of the different kind of literacy at work relative to each—print-linguistic text and image, though both represent communication systems (Murray, 2009).

In the past fifteen years, another focus of study within literacy studies has emerged that focuses on the use of multiple modes to communicate and related practices. Studies pertaining to this analysis seek to understand rhetorical attributes of mixed modes and when and under what conditions certain combinations are most productive (e.g., Lemke, 1998 and 1999; and Richards, 2003). Murray indicates that because of connections between language and consciousness a given combination may be meaningful for some people while the same combination will not be as productive for others because of differing backgrounds that include not just literacy training, but literacy experiences and understanding of the universe (p. 16). Indeed, several theories of multimodality and this relationship between print-linguistic text and image have been presented, but each seems to have its own difficulties meeting the challenges of theory development thereof.

An example I used in *HTB* is that of Kress and Van Leeuwen (2001). They attempt to develop a theory of semiotics that integrates terminology describing various rhetorical dynamics at work in multimodal forms of communication. They recognize the relationship between composer and "reader" as an interactive one; the reader acts upon a message as much as a composer initiates it. Furthermore, they articulate that the message is not just the content but its form relative to how it is presented and the communicators' relationship to each other and their experiences. The terminology they use includes: discourse, design, production, and distribution (pp. 4–5). Discourse pertains to socially constructed knowledge. Design pertains to the resources that one uses to create meaning. A diagram of an object represents a different kind of visual representation than does a photograph of the same object; a diagram will integrate labels and dimension information, providing details that a photograph may not be able to provide. Design frames how meaning is made. Production describes the materiality of the expression, the media used to make the message visible/material. A print-linguistic document is able to provide information a certain way; however, a video demonstration presents the same information in another way, while a real-time, in person demonstration facilitates information yet a third way. Distribution, similar to the fifth rhetorical canon of delivery, refers to the means by which readers access the material message (pp. 20–21). Multimodal presentation is facilitated through a system that affects meaning-making: how people of a given community understand language (discourse), how people understand certain conventions of communication (design), how people use certain tools to develop a given message or artifact of communication (production), and how people disseminate those artifacts. All of which are affected by available technologies.

They also apply certain terms to explain the social interaction involved in making meaning. "Mode" pertains to the different "genres" of composition identified by the New London Group, of which Kress is a member. These include aural, visual, print-linguistic, experiential, and spatial as well as combinations. The term "medium" pertains to the material resources used to produce a message. "Experiential meaning potential" is a term that pertains to the roles that peoples' past experiences play in contributing to making meaning out of a given message. One who has only learned how to do new tasks through demonstration and practice and has never used a print-linguistic document will not understand how to use a manual to learn a new process. Finally, "provenance" pertains to the importing of certain signs into different contexts to help people understand each other's ideas and values (pp. 21–23).

Much of the literature in cognitive neuroscience on persuasion pertains to the integration of different sensory experiences toward facilitating persuasion—how neurons react to stimuli and how different modes of representation and different sensory experiences related to those modes interact with each other neurologically to affect persuasion and perception. While some studies focus on questions pertaining to development of particular neuro-processing combinations and how different modalities are processed, some studies consider the development of this integration itself. Much of this book revolves around the studies pertaining to how neurons interact around the brain during certain tasks, not on the development of this integration. However, I want to point out that the Gestalt effect is identified in much of the scholarship on visual rhetoric, especially (Arnheim, 1969); yet, it is also included as a term/ concept in the neuroscience scholarship (Wallace, 2004). Wallace states broadly that one of the roles of the brain "is to synthesize this mélange of sensory information into an adaptive and coherent perceptual Gestalt... this sensory synthesis is a constantly occurring phenomenon that is continually shaping our view of the world" (p. 625). I review some of the literature from neurobiology regarding various modal combinations and how they are described in that scholarship. This discussion omits studies pertaining to demonstrating cognition, which involves another dynamic of neural process. For example, studies have found that the neural activity related to deciding to do a particular action precedes the display of that action (Massumi, 2002).

A few studies find that as an optimal combination of senses is engaged the brain is able to process the information faster (Bremner and Spence, 2008; Keetels and Vroomen, 2012; and Lewkowicz and Kraebel, 2004). They study how the neurons process information relative to the temporal synchronicity of the sensory experiences. That is, they consider the amount of time that passes between receiving visual information and auditory information or other modes engaging different senses.

While the general understanding is that the less time that passes between the two senses are engaged simultaneously the better able the brain is to process both bits of information, they question the time needed to process different combinations and the rate at which each mode or sense can be engaged optimally. Just as sound travels slower than light, Keetels and Vroomen (2012) acknowledge that, "[t]he neural processing time also differs between the senses, and it is typically slower for visual than for auditory stimuli" (p. 148).

The rest of this chapter summarizes attributes of particular modal combinations relative to cognitive neuroscience.

Neuro-rhetoric of Particular Senses

Visual-Dominance Effect

There is much literature about visual rhetoric. Visual representations occur in many forms and are prevalent, especially in persuasive rhetoric. This integration is detailed in other chapters in this book as specific examples are discussed. Advertisements rarely include only print-linguistic text; they include a combination of text and at least one image of the product or service provided.

Indeed, Arnheim (1969), Mitchell (1995), and Pinker (1997) argue for examination of visual representations and how the mind processes them. Images are important to one's cognitive understanding of abstract ideas and concepts and the relationship of image to text (Arnheim, 1969; and Mitchell, 1995). While Arnheim values image over words, Mitchell conveys equality between the two suggesting that value of one over the other depends on context.

Arnheim (1969) was among the earliest scholars to argue for the value of images to facilitate cognition. While print-linguistic text had been emphasized generally (as also evidenced in the historical study), visuals carry with them what Arnheim calls a "Gestalt effect." Visuals can be seen in their entirety, while words must be processed individually, breaking up flow of information. Arnheim's main point is that in order to best accommodate cognition through visual perception, pictures need to articulate meaning explicitly or link closely to the reader's prior experiences to facilitate meaning-making; "Pictures and films will be aids only if they meet the requirements of visual thinking" (p. 308).

Mitchell (1995) also observes that images can be read various ways, and they interact with words various ways as well. He alludes to the concept of "Ekphrasis"—that one can state a given message using various combinations of image and text together. The concept of multimodal rhetoric suggests that authors of multimodal works need to try to find ways to combine the various modes available—not just words and images, but possibly audio and space among others—to accomplish a given purpose most effectively and efficiently.

One of Mayer's (2001) multimodal principles, which integrates attributes of Pinker's theory, is that people may attempt to "build a visual model" if one is not provided. However, they may not attempt to do so, or the visual model they construct may be erroneous. If a picture is provided, people can make the visual connection more readily (pp. 72–78). For example, I detailed several attributes of the Training Within Industry program, a program associated with the current lean operations philosophy and which integrates several elements of multimodality (Remley, 2014). I showed in that book how the Training Within Industry program's modeling for developing a proposal toward process improvement ("Job Methods") encourages the proposer to include, in addition to textual descriptions, a diagram of the current process to show any problems in it and then include a diagram of the proposed process to show how it addresses those problems and increases efficiency (pp. 143–153). One can even integrate a bar graph to visually represent any quantifiable benefits of the proposed process (time difference to complete a single unit, difference in production or potential profit).

It is generally recognized in neuroscience scholarship that vision is the dominant modality in humans (Colavita, 1974; Howard and Templeton, 1966; and Welch and Warren, 1986). Spence, Parise, and Chen (2012) describe the neurological basis for this apparent favoring of the visual over other modes of representation. They review literature on the Colavita visual dominance effect, which recognizes that visual stimuli tend to get a stronger response from neurons than other stimuli. Colavita (1974) found, in a series of four experiments, that subjects responded to visual stimuli before they responded to any other sensory stimulus

(p. 411). Further, he notes that scholarship generally recognizes that people "do not respond as effectively to two simultaneously presented stimuli as to the same two stimuli presented in succession" (p. 412). However, Spence, Parise, and Chen suggest that this effect is attributable to the fact that the visual information is received, generally, before any other information—auditory or touch, for example (p. 537). Because vision is the first sense that receives information it, naturally, is engaged immediately; though, auditory information is actually processed faster than visual information.

Other studies suggest that the other senses do not adequately compensate for the absence of visual senses, for example, in people with low vision or blindness, negatively affecting learning abilities (Elmer, 2004; and Pasqualotto and Proulx, 2012). Donahue, Woldorff, and Mitroff (2010) report that video game players tend to have refined visual attention and visual perception abilities, contributing to enhanced multisensory processing ability.

Visual rhetoric has received a lot of attention; however, other senses come into play in cognition as well. Most of it recognizes the esteem given to visual attributes. Neuroscience recognizes the value of visual modes in facilitating cognition; however, it also finds that other senses contribute to the learning processes as well. One of the most-studied combinations is the visual-auditory combination.

Visual-Auditory Links

The auditory cortex is the portion of the brain where most of our auditory (hearing) processing occurs. Neuroscience scholarship explains this benefit in the linkage of visual stimuli being processed within the auditory cortex. According to Bizley and King (2012), "more than one quarter of the neurons associated with the auditory cortex are influenced by visual stimuli" (p. 37). They go on to state that visual stimuli enhance the processing that occurs in the auditory cortex. In particular, they state that visual inputs can increase the sensitivity and selectivity of responses to auditory information (p. 40). This is supported in other studies as well (Kajikawa et al., 2012; Kayser et al., 2012; Munhall and Vatikiotis-Bateson, 2004; and Newell, 2004). Newell suggests that auditory information complements visual information to help refine one's understanding of the information; likewise, visual information may facilitate refinement of auditory information, as when one hears a siren from afar, and then sees a fire truck (as opposed to a police car). The visual of the fire truck helps the person understand that a fire-related emergency is occurring. Linguistic scholarship generally observes that one benefits from facial expressions (a visual stimulus) as non-verbal cues when one is speaking (auditory) to them. Bernstein, Auer, and Moore (2004), though, identify some debate regarding whether this relationship is one of convergence (facilitated by multimodal neurons—information-processing occurring at same time with same neurons) or association (neurons of two different modalities being used to process different kinds of information). They conclude that it is one of association (p. 218).

However, scholarship in neuroscience also indicates that the auditory sensory experience can affect visual perception related to other modalities, including space, time, and motion (Shams, Kamitani, and Shimojo, 2004). So, while one experiences visual information, other senses can affect how that information is perceived.

Previous Experience

Steven Pinker (1997) acknowledges that the mind works as a system that includes one's prior experiences and various forms of representation to understand information. We retain images of various objects and our interactions with the world to assist in understanding future interactions with those objects or people and situations that may be similar. Fields such as distributed cognition and social semiotics theorize the relationship between social interactions and cognitive processes.

How one perceives the world is very much a function of the influence others may have on them. Teachers and parents exert considerable influence in shaping a child's perception of the world; children learn how to think about the world by watching adults perform tasks and listening to someone tell them about the world. Any biases one has about the world can be transferred to a child whom he or she is teaching. Further, our values are socially constructed, which influences how we perceive the value of a given product or service or policy.

Distinguishing artificial intelligence from human intelligence, Brooks and Stein (1994) note that human "intelligence cannot be separated from subjective experience of a body" (p. 7). Even Schiappa (2003) argues the multiplicity of reality. What one perceives as "reality" is established through their interaction with the world. Such interaction involves experiences one has by himself as well as interactions with others that help to shape our understanding of our experiences. Two people who come from very different backgrounds may have different perceptions of the world, and this affects how they interpret information. Much scholarship in social semiotics and multimodality also observes this relationship, and scholarship in neurobiology and cognitive neuroscience also recognizes the role of previous experience in cognition.

This study of the role of previous experience in cognition is important because persuasion is affected by one's perceptions of the world. A model that recognizes and considers this role and one's prior learning experiences may facilitate development of more effective learning tools.

Relative to the concept of distributed cognition, Hutchins (2000) notes that "something special might be happening in systems of distributed processing, whether the processors are neurons, connectionist nodes, areas of a brain, whole persons, groups of persons, or groups of groups of persons" (p. 2). As systems interact new knowledge is developed and cognition occurs. This knowledge development and cognition may be relative to the individual—neuron-processing, or to an entire culture—processing that occurs among groups of groups of persons, and any level in between. That is, distributed cognition can be at the level of the individual (distribution of systems within the brain) or at the level of culture (p. 5).

Hutchins also recalls Vygotsky's (1986) points that cognitive function occurs at two levels—interpsychological and intrapsychological. Drawing on Vygotsky and socially distributed cognition, Hutchins acknowledges that, "the new functional system inside the child is brought into existence in the interaction of the child with others (typically adults) and with artifacts" (p. 5). Further, it is through these interactions that one can eventually learn to understand a situation "in the absence of the others" (p. 5). Neural plasticity facilitates this cognitive development within the individual's brain, but social interaction is a part of that neural development. Finally, Hutchins notes the contextual nature of cognition. He observes that "cognitive activity is sometimes situated in the material world in such a way that the environment is a computational medium" (p. 7).

Further, as Mayer (2001) does, Gee (2003) connects prior experience and cognition. People learn by making connections between past experiences and new experiences (pp. 75–76). These experiences can affect how ready one is to change their perception of something toward action relative to a persuasive message. Much as Moreno and Mayer (2000) observe that different people may respond differently to training because of their background experiences, Lacey and Sathian (2012) observe that, "individual history (visual experience, training, etc.)" can affect how each person responds to various sensory experiences (p. 184). Other neuroscientists also note the role of experience in understanding how information is processed (King, Doubell, and Skaliora, 2004; and Wallace, 2004).

Conclusion

There is considerable overlap in understanding what affects cognition relative to the various scientific fields involved in cognition—social, natural, and physical. As Jack (2012) observes with her introduction of the concept of "neurorhetoric," the field of rhetoric can contribute to studies in cognitive neuroscience. The information I have provided here, showing these overlaps, helps to introduce a model that can facilitate interdisciplinary theorization and study specific to multimodal rhetoric and cognition. In the next chapters I detail the model that can be used to integrate the two disciplines.

3 The Neuro-Cognitive Model of Multimodal Rhetoric

In this chapter I review specific attributes of a neuro-cognitive model of multimodal rhetoric that I first proposed in *HTB* to which I have referred (2015). However, I apply it to persuasive multimodal messages. Considering the review of extant literature in both fields—neurobiology/ physiology and multimodal rhetoric—provided in the previous chapter, five particular characteristics of neurobiology, distributed cognition, and multimodal rhetoric emerge, each of which integrates elements of existing theory; however, I synthesize perspectives from both fields. Again, much of this chapter is a review of a similar chapter from *HTB*.

A debate in the field of multimodal rhetoric is the orientation of a given theory. As mentioned in Chapter 1, rhetoric includes the way information is presented within a message (design of a message) and how one perceives that message (audience's perception of the information in the message). Kress' terminology, for example, tends to focus on design attributes of multimodality; items that affect how one is able to develop a given multimodal product and how one considers that product via social semiotics. Others like Ball (2006) and Odell and Katz (2009) try to theorize more from the audience's perspective; that is, how to develop a given message relative to how one perceives information and their expectations relative to information needs. Much like the process of usability testing in technical communication and information architecture, Remley (2012) attempts to use both approaches as a means to develop good products through an interactive and iterative process; a multimodal object is developed and tested, an audience provides feedback regarding their perception of that object and its ability to help them understand its meaning toward facilitating revision to improve the rhetorical effectiveness; that is, to improve the ability of the message to provide the intended meaning so the audience can understand it better.

Because this theory integrates biological and social attributes it is, necessarily, audience-oriented; however, it attempts to integrate attributes of design. As is generally considered within the field of professional communication, one must understand one's audience and its information needs before designing a given message. So, this model can be applied relative to analyzing a given product and an audiences' reaction to its effectiveness as well as relative to designing an effective product to facilitate cognition.

The five particular attributes from a synthesis of scholarship in multimodal rhetoric and neurobiology that emerge are:

1   Inter-modal sensory redundancy—the preference to integrate more than one sense to facilitate re-enforcement of information;
2   Visual dominance—recognition that the visual sense is usually engaged first, and as such is dominant in information processing;
3   Temporal synchronicity—the timing of exposure to different stimuli affects how related information is processed;
4   Prior experience—the role that previous experience with certain information or learning style has on acquiring new information; and
5   Attention-modal filtering—that one must filter certain modal information in an effort to concentrate and best process relevant multimodal information.

Any multimodal message or multisensory experience integrates all of these attributes towards affecting perception of information. While it appears to involve more attributes of neurobiology than social science, certain attributes of social semiotic theory are captured throughout this model. The media through which social interactions are facilitated contribute to developing neural structures that support, or not, all of the attributes in this model. Mitchell (1995) observed that we are a visual culture; it is not a coincidence when one considers the prominence of visual stimuli in various media available since 1990: television, Internet, conference calls. Even radio has entered the visual field with some shows being broadcast on television.

Research can focus on any one or combination of two or more of these attributes. Scholarship in visual rhetoric, for example, has focused on elements of visual dominance while emphasizing social semiotic theories—the impact that our relationships have on our understanding and processing of visual information. However, with this integrated model it can also consider inclusion of the Colavita visual dominance effect—a biological phenomenon. However, I develop the discussion of research approaches in another chapter. In this chapter I want to detail each of the model's attributes. First, I need to clarify some terms I use within this discussion. Because I am integrating discourse from different fields, some terms from each need to be explained and reconciled.

The Role of Motivation and Reward in Persuasion

An intrinsic variable that influences some cognition, including persuasion and perception of the world, is that of motivation. An audience that is motivated toward change is easier to persuade than one that is not motivated toward change. Motivation is linked to rewards.

When a person perceives a reward to exist with performing or doing well on a given task they are more motivated to pursue that task. Attaining the reward makes them feel good; so, they want to do that task. A student may perceive teacher or parental-approval to be a reward. In fact, one may perceive any of the following as rewards: earned points, good grades, improved chances of getting a job or raise, potential for advancement in a workplace, or any of many other short or long-term rewards. There are neurons that facilitate an understanding of reward linking with motivation. These are labeled as "reward neurons" or "dopamine neurons" (Arias-Carrion and Poppel, 2007; Hueske, 2011; and Schultz, Apicella, and Ljungberg, 1993). They exist in the mid-brain, where much synthesizing of stimuli occurs. Consequently, it is important to consider their inclusion with any neuro-scientific model of cognition.

Reward neurons release dopamine, a chemical that facilitates transmission of messages/impulses between synapses. Dopamine is also synthesized in various pharmaceutical drugs to address certain neural-blocking disorders such as Parkinson's Disease (MacDonald et al., 2011), and non-pharmaceutical drugs associated with a "high" or "happy" feeling such as methamphetamine and cocaine enhance the effect of these neurons (Venton et al., 2006). While these neurons are not involved in processing modal stimuli, they do play a role in learning and persuasion.

Terminology

Certain terminology is associated with the attributes that I mention. I exclude the concept of the reward neurons; because they may be applied implicitly or explicitly, and I describe some application of them with different cases. However, the terms I list here are integrated into the design of multimodal instructional materials and activities. Some of these are consistent across the disciplinary discourses related to the model. The principle terms that require some explanation are:

1   modal or mode
2   sensory or sense
3   filtering
4   processing

Generally, they are used consistently between the discourse communities involved; however, I briefly explain each to eliminate any potential confusion.

Modal/Modes: As defined by the New London Group (1996), a mode is a particular system of representation. It is the particular means through which particular neurons are stimulated. That is, visual modes stimulate visual neurons of either uni-modal or multi-modal types. Modal is an adjective that pertains to a given mode or representation system that acts as a stimulus.

Sensory/Sense: Neuro-physiological activity is generally described relative to cortices associated with the senses that are stimulated by particular modes of representation. A sense is the biological experience associated with a given stimulus. For example, visual modes stimulate neurons associated with the visual sense. Sensory is an adjective related to sense. Visual sensory experience, for example, pertains to the experience associated with the visual sense.

Filtering: To filter means to distinguish between relevant and irrelevant information. As one experiences particular information he or she must consider whether that information is relevant to a given message. If certain information is perceived as relevant the brain concentrates on that information so it becomes part of the cognitive process. Information perceived as irrelevant is removed from further consideration within a cognitive process. However, that act of removing the information is part of a cognitive process.

Processing: Because neural dynamics are associated with the model, the term processing pertains to that activity. That is, it pertains directly to the behaviors of neurons toward facilitating cognition. I use the term "cognitive processing" several times; this term pertains to the behaviors of neurons as they facilitate cognition based on responses to stimuli.

Again, most of the terms are used consistently in scholarship from the different disciplines involved; however, this information re-enforces their definitions within this theory. I explain each attribute of the model in the following sections of this chapter.

Inter-Modal Sensory Redundancy

Moreno and Mayer (2000) theorized a redundancy principle relative to integrating similar information in two modal forms in a single message to re-enforce the information. The same kind of principle applies to the theory of multimodal neuron processing. Bizley and King (2012) describe the visual-auditory link and how auditory information helps to process visual information, and both can be facilitated via multimodal neurons. Newell (2004) echoes this finding. A basic principle of cognition is the re-enforcement of information. This model recognizes this re-enforcement with this principle.

Generally, it appears that neurons associated with the first sense engaged attempt to process information toward cognition; however, they want more senses involved. This may be why multimodal neurons exist and become active with sensory information from various modes of representation. Multimodal neurons facilitate processing multimodal information, which, as Arnheim (1969) explains, facilitates a Gestalt effect—a more complete picture of the information. Further, many neurons seem to converge in a portion of the mid-brain (Clemo, Keniston, and Meredith, 2012; and King and Calvert, 2001). Neurons of all types— unimodal and multimodal—intersect or come to a point where they seem to intersect (Clemo, Keniston, and Meredith, p. 5). While different cortices are associated with particular stimuli, the neurons all follow paths into the mid-brain. Clemo et al. report on studies of cats and monkeys, but they generalize these findings to humans.

The initial neurons engaged processes information, but other modal neurons re-enforce or further define information, much as theorized by Moreno and Mayer (2000). For example, visual information shows what an object/abstract concept is or looks like. Other modes contribute to refining definition or composition of the object. In the example provided by Moreno and Mayer—learning about lightning—an image of a house, clouds, and lightning are provided, and text labels various attributes of the process involved in generating lightning. The pictures of the objects facilitate some information, but without the text it would be difficult to comprehend the process fully. The study group related to the animation and narration combination (visual-audio) was better able to learn information than was the group that had animation and text (strictly visual).

It also re-enforces what Mitchell (1995) states about "ekphrasis." The concept related to optimal combinations of modes toward best articulating a message. Information related to a single sense can facilitate cognition; however, information from various modes facilitates cognition better. Perrault, Rowland, and Stein (2012) call this "multi-sensory enhancement" or "multi-sensory synergy." Connecting neurophysiology to behavior, they observe that multisensory inputs tend to "elicit more vigorous responses than are evoked by the strongest of them individually" (p. 281).

This principle is echoed throughout the cases presented in subsequent chapters. For example, Chapter 5 discusses it relative to simulators and how they engage visual as well as tactile and spatial senses. Flight simulators, specifically, place a student pilot in the environment in which he or she would operate and allows that student to experience all the sensory stimuli a pilot flying a particular aircraft would experience.

Visual Dominance

There is a plethora of empirical data related to visual processing and visual rhetoric. An entire subfield within both areas of rhetoric and neurobiology works with this scholarship. Much of it pertains to relationships between visual information and combinations with other senses. Arnheim (1969) and Mitchell (1996) emphasize the visual attributes of cognition, even in the titles of their respective texts—*Visual Thinking* and *Picture Theory*. While most of this attribute comes from neurobiology, some dynamics are recognized in both neurobiology and social semiotic theory.

Again, neurobiology scholarship finds an attention-related preference for visual information. If visual information exists along with other stimuli, then the visual will draw attention no matter what other stimuli are involved. Generally, the first sense engaged has priority in processing information. However, the visual is perceived before any other stimulus, which affects perception of effects of various modes. According to Spence, Parise, and Chen (2012) studies related to varying the timing of exposure to audio and visual stimuli and awareness of one being perceived before the other find that only when audio stimuli are presented at least 600 milliseconds before the visual stimulus is presented do participants perceive the audio to precede the visual. When multiple stimuli are involved at approximately the same time and vision is one of them, the visual will be attended to more than any other stimulus. Spence, Parise, and Chen (2012) note that scholarship on the Colavita visual dominance effect finds that even if one is directed to attend to audio stimuli when the two—visual and audio—are provided at the same time, one attends primarily to the visual (p. 534). They also note that if the presentation of audio stimuli precedes visual stimuli, that can affect the degree to which one attends to visual stimuli (p. 534). Regardless, they state that, "although attentional manipulations can sometimes be used to modulate, or even eliminate, the Colavita visual dominance effect, they cannot be used to reverse it" (p. 534). Once the visual sense is integrated, attention to that stimulus will persist.

In the absence of direct visual stimuli, one tends to imagine or looks for an equivalent based on engaged senses. As Mayer (2001) observed, one may "attempt to build a visual model" (p. 63). When one is talking to someone else on the telephone he may envision the person with whom he is speaking if they are acquainted. If listening to a radio broadcast, one may try to recall a picture of the radio personality who is talking or a photograph of the band if listening to music. This re-enforces the modal redundancy principle; one wants as much stimuli to help process information. If the visual stimulus is absent, the brain will attempt to create a visual stimulus to assist cognition. One remembers what the person looks like from previous interactions and experiences with them and envisions them.

Visual multimodal neurons dominate because more information is contained in visual information than other senses. There is an appeal about the Gestalt effect, identified by Arnheim (1969). One can assess spatial relations, textures, size, distance, proportions, and image within just visual information. While other senses may provide refinement of the assessment related to those items, multiple types of visual information are provided in one image.

Social science research has theorized how interactions and technologies through which they occur affect perception and cognition. I discuss the influence that technology has in the next chapter; however, I describe relevant theories associated with the visual dominance attribute of the model here. Media technologies that facilitate visual information/visual forms of information encourage visual dominance effect, also facilitating "visual culture." For example, two particular theories of communication technology are ideal for integrating social semiotics into the discussion. These are "Media Richness Theory" and "Social Presence Theory."

Media Richness Theory argues that given media will facilitate effective communication for a given task. Different media are required for different tasks because of the level of richness or ability to minimize uncertainty or ambiguity (Bouwman et al., 2005; and Rice, 1993). Traditional face-to-face communication is considered the richest medium. The listener is able to see the communicator's visual cues and hear voice inflections that help to understand a message, while the speaker is able to see the listener's reaction and respond to any potential confusion immediately. Potential for confusion is limited because of the multiple stimuli available to assist in cognition.

Similarly, Social Presence Theory considers the degree to which communicators feel the other is "present" while communicating. Generally, it is perceived that more "social" communication can occur when communicators are physically present to each other, as in face-to-face communication; while more formal communication is likely to occur when that physical presence is lacking, as in e-mail (Hewett, Remley, Zemliansky, and DiPardo, 2010). Social Presence Theory attempts to understand to what degree certain media facilitate social presence, and therefore, more effective communication. In both theories the ability to see and hear one conveying a message is considered the best to facilitate cognition. I consider this aspect of the general model more in a subsequent chapter.

Video tutorials are a popular form of instructional tool for asynchronous learning. Such videos allow a viewer to see the narrator or the task being taught in the absence of a real face-to-face interaction with the teacher or trainer. Commercials tend to integrate video and narration; so, a similar dynamic occurs relative to persuasive communication.

Related to this intersection of visual rhetoric, technology, and cognition is that medical scans contribute to cognition about a condition and shape medical decisions. Teston (2012) observes within deliberations about cancer-patient care that "the visual makes possible the construction of knowledge about disease" (p. 205). Even within the medical field, decisions are being made based on visual information, re-enforcing the powerful role played by visual stimuli and technologies that closely reproduce the material.

Again, scholarship in visual rhetoric and neurobiology recognize the preference and esteem associated with visual modes and sense. That neurobiology recognizes biological attributes that account for it can help advance our understanding of multimodal rhetoric.

Temporal Synchronicity

Per studies by Keetels and Vrooman (2012) and Moreno and Mayer (2000), sensory information is processed at different rates. Neurons are able to process sensory information at different rates relative to the modes involved. While the Colavita visual dominance effect recognizes this, it emphasizes any combinations that include visual modes. The principle of temporal synchronicity considers combinations in any modal form, including those that use the same mode such as two forms of visual information—print-linguistic text and video, for example. Such an issue is important to a theory of cognition because the rate at which information can be processed affects the rate at which cognition may occur. Multimodal rhetoric involves ascertaining optimal combinations of modes to facilitate cognition.

Moreno and Mayer had four different modal combinations relative to timing of the information. In their studies, they found that when information from visual and auditory modes was processed at the same time, learners were able to acquire information better than when the same kind of information was facilitated via two kinds of visual information at the same time (animation and text). However, they also found that learners tended to transfer knowledge better when they learned via a sequence of different modal information—watching an animation and then hearing a narration about what they viewed.

Such findings indicate that the types of modes involved and timing of information provided affect the efficiency of processing it. As mentioned above, when audio stimuli are presented several milliseconds before the visual stimulus is presented, participants perceive that the audio precedes the visual. Consequently, timing of exposure associated with certain modal combinations becomes part of the rhetorical effectiveness of those combinations. As considered with the Colavita visual dominance effect, the visual is the fastest sense engaged, but it takes the longest to process information. However, sound takes less time to process. When both visual and auditory senses are stimulated, both are attended to by the audience. Perhaps this influences the first attribute stated above—inter-modal redundancy and the desire for more senses to be engaged in cognition. That is, combining senses to help facilitate cognition enables the system to process information faster. As indicated earlier, though, the timing of sensory engagement or modal presentation can affect the degree to which particular neurons are engaged and, consequently, how information is processed (Spence, Parise, and Chen, 2012).

Also, head injuries and brain disorders that affect the various cortices impact how the brain can process information. Consequently, scholarship in neurobiology/physiology is considering more precisely how such injuries and disorders affect what may be considered effective rhetorical combinations within learning and perception generally. Examples of such research include: autism; brain injuries; lost or low vision; deafness; and neurological disorder or injury that causes numbing of touch sensory experience. As mentioned in the previous chapter, neuro-physiological scholarship finds that combinations of visual and touch senses contribute to understanding how to interact with physical objects; if one can hold an object but not feel it, how would that impact one's perception of it?

Prior Experience

Scholarship associated with the general field of cognition observes that prior experience plays a major role in learning. As mentioned in Chapter 2, prominent works by Pinker, Gee, Moreno, and Mayer and Hutchins echo this understanding about learning. Unless affected by memory disorders, one cannot help but learn from experience. As one experiences a given situation, he or she recalls a similar experience and consequences associated with their actions related to it. If he did not like the outcome of his actions, he reflects on what he could have done differently and changes his behavior accordingly to try to get a better outcome the next time it occurs. With each experience, one changes their actions to try to arrive at a favorable outcome related to the experience. This is the process of learning to behave a certain way to bring about a given outcome relative to a particular context or situation. These situations, though, tend to be social; so, this attribute involves much social science. However, it also influences neurons, because neurons grow synapses with each social experience that re-enforces certain information or knowledge. The more synapses one has developed from previous experiences and learning, the faster one can process related information.

Spence, Parise, and Chen (2012) and Lacey and Sathian (2012), also, study how prior experience affects neuro-physiological processes. They find, generally, that experience contributes to changing neurological behaviors (plasticity). Plasticity is a lifelong process; different kinds of changes occur at different periods of one's life. Hoiland (2012) notes that neurons grow in developmental years and some die out as we age. Gopnick et al. (1999) assert that there are approximately 2500 synapses per neuron at birth; this grows to approximately 15,000 synapses per neuron by the time one is 3 years old. However, the average adult has only about 7500 synapses per neuron. Experience dictates which synapses are deleted or "pruned" (Gopnick et al.,1999). Generally, as one learns a given task, more synaptic links of certain types develop, facilitating faster processing of information. Clemo, Keniston, and Meredith (2012) report that in their studies of monkeys and cats the average number of synaptic connections for a single neuron is two to three; but some may have as many as four connections (p. 11). As one learns from experience, more connections are developed for each related synapse, and these connections help to process information faster.

Such changes to neurons, stimulated by patterns of learning approaches, contribute to affecting perception and attention attributes of information processing. Consequently, this attribute can involve analyses of plasticity and synaptic connections. Such dynamics may also affect whether one is visual learner or less so; what instructional/learning methods has person been exposed to earlier in life/development? Is one able to process information conveyed via radio transmission as readily as one experiences a television broadcast? One who has a lot of experience watching sporting events on television but has rarely experienced a radio broadcast of a sports event, for example, may not be able to follow a radio broadcast. Radio broadcast of sports events involves imagining action based on description; television facilitates both visual and audio information.

As suggested with the references to Gee and Mitchell, learning via social interactions affects what is learned and how. This is another area where social science theories contribute to the integrated theory. As Hutchins (2000) noted, distributed cognition involves any system, whether it be neural systems or systems of groups of people (p. 2). Hutchins also acknowledges that it is through interactions with artifacts as well as with others that cognitive development occurs (p. 5). Such interactions affect neural plasticity within the individual's brain; social interaction is a part of that neural development. It is generally recognized that learning occurs through experience. The hippocampus stores memories of previous experiences; so, it may be included within consideration of prior experiences.

Culture is a social phenomenon; so, visual culture is a social valuing of visual information. However, social elements of technology also are involved in the use of technologies—visual/audio/other—including simulators. Gee and Mitchell separately note the increased use of simulators for training purposes, and a subfield of scholarship in cognition examines such uses of simulators and related technologies. Remley (2009) also notes the use of hands-on training to help people transition to new kinds of work using a training approach similar to what they received previously. Such scholarship finds that when people learn how to do particular tasks a certain way and that way has been used throughout their lives for learning new tasks, people are more likely to favor that approach, be it visual, hands-on, or otherwise.

Culture also shapes our values; what we perceive as a reward, punishment; and what we value about other people and why we want to be like them or not. Consequently, prior experience also contributes to development of reward neurons and mirror neurons.

Finally, prior experience helps us to understand what we should fear and what we do not need to fear. Our amygdala naturally signals to us that something should be feared because it challenges our survival; however, experience with that something can eliminate that perception. We learn not to fear it through experiences.

Our prior experiences contribute to shaping our understanding and ways we come to understand new concepts. This principle recognizes the role of that experience in cognition.

Attention-Modal Filtering

The last attribute of the integrated model pertains to the literature about filtering of information and attention. Moreno and Mayer describe the attention principle related to learning with multimodal tools. When irrelevant information is included in the information, it negatively affects cognition; the brain must process too much information, and it has to filter what it perceives to be relevant and what it perceives to be irrelevant. The more modes there are involved, the more challenging this is. Further, they recognize the Baddeley (1986) principle of short term memory and its ability to process information. That is, the more modes there are involved, the more processes are involved, and that negatively affects the ability to process information. Baddeley and Moreno and Mayer encourage limiting modes to two.

Tufte (2006) also observes that irrelevant information negatively affects the ability to understand a given message. He terms such information "chart-junk." Generally, it is textual or visual information that is not required within a given image or graphic in order to understand the meaning of that graphic. Its inclusion gives the initial impression that it is relevant, and the brain attempts to process it. Consequently, the filtering process related to ascertaining which information is relevant and which is not slows down cognition. This effect on the brain and cognition is observed in neurobiological/physiological scholarship.

Campos and Bulthoff (2012) find this relationship relative to virtual environments: the less irrelevant information that is contained in a message, the better one is able to process it quickly. Irrelevant stimuli must be filtered to get to relevant information. So, re-enforcing scholarship in cognitive psychology and education, the more one can eliminate irrelevant information the faster one can process the information, contributing to better learning.

Medium

The principles described so far are part of the design of the message relative to how it facilitates neural processes toward cognition. The rhetorical situation includes consideration of the audience, purpose, and medium or media used to convey the message. Neural attributes are part of the consideration of the audience, and the purpose within the parameters of this book is instruction. The model considers the medium of delivery as a framing attribute. In multimodal rhetoric the medium engages multiple senses. Cognition involves multiple senses, and various media engage multiple senses through the modes of representation they use. Consequently, the medium or media used for delivering the message influence what stimuli can be used within the instructional message. A given medium facilitates or restricts the stimuli used for instruction, affecting neural processing, too. Consequently, part of the discussion I present reflects a critique of the technological tools associated with the product used in the case study chapters.

I use cases associated with a number of different media—face-to-face interaction, multiple forms of video, simulation, and slide shows. The technology associated with the media shapes the message, and one needs to consider affordances and constraints of a given tool to develop an effective message. I detail this consideration in Chapter 4.

Figure 3.1 represents this model visually. Each attribute is represented; though not in any particular ordering. The model integrates elements of the multimodal product/composition, but it focuses attention on the product's ability to engage an audience's neurological experiences and perceptions of information toward cognition. Different combinations of modes provided in a given piece, affected by the technology available with the media, are the objects of study relative to all but "prior experience." Inter-modal sensory redundancy examines the particular combinations at work and their resulting sensory experiences. Visual dominance suggests the degree to which the visual mode is dominant in a given piece, prompting the visual sensory experience. Temporal synchronicity studies the timing of presentation and how that timing affects perception and processes. Modal-Attention Filtering examines the degree to which one distinguishes between relevant and irrelevant information and filters out what he or she perceives to be irrelevant and why.

Each attribute is represented independently because each can be studied as a unit of analysis in itself. That is, each may be isolated within an analysis while others are maintained relative to the product or audience. However, it is important to understand that all contribute to cognitive processes. Further, because various dynamics occur within each attribute, one may study a set of dynamics, much as social semiotic scholarship has tended to focus on the social attributes of, for example, prior experience. So, existing scholarship can still fit into this model.

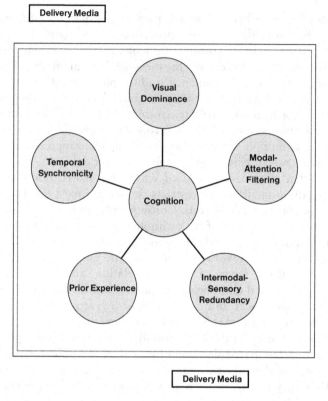

Figure 3.1 Model.

Surrounding the attributes described above is the medium used for delivery, which frames the message and shapes the means by which cognition can occur. I detail the frame in the next chapter. Each attribute, then, represents an attribute of the message that engages neurological and semiotic dynamics that facilitate cognition.

Studying Multimodal Rhetoric Through the Socio-neurobiological Lens

As mentioned in previous chapters, the fields of rhetoric and neurobiology/physiology tend to examine multimodal and multisensory experiences differently, using different tools especially. While rhetoric studies tend to focus attention on composition and observed behaviors or surveys of audience perception of content, neurophysiological studies focus on particular neuron behaviors inside the brain based on biomedical technologies. However, these neurobiological/physiological studies involve analysis of such activity relative to certain stimuli; nevertheless, social science is involved in neurobiology/physiology. As such, this model can also be applied to rhetorical analyses of multimodal products/stimuli to form a neurorhetorical analysis. Consequently, rhetorical theory, often linked with social sciences, can contribute to cognitive neuroscience studies; and the field of rhetoric can benefit from integrated studies likewise.

Examples of potential studies include ascertaining how the brain processes certain modal combinations; rhetoric scholars can design these combinations. Studies can triangulate data by including both biomedical technologies as well as social science research methods such as surveys and interviews with participants as well as observation and quasi-experimental designs. I discuss such studies in later chapters. However, the chapters immediately following this one detail neurorhetorical analyses of specific products without triangulation.

Theoretical Limitations

A limitation of this model is that it assumes a reasonably normal neurobiology/physiology is at work; however, it also facilitates theory development relative to neural disorders or the absence of certain neurophysiological elements. As mentioned above, numerous studies in neurophysiology consider the biology associated with low-vision or blindness and relative to other disorders. Such disorders suggest damage to the cognitive system referred to in Chapter 1. The brain compensates for what it lacks to facilitate cognition; however, such disorders present challenges to understanding how neural processes work in damaged systems.

An example of such a limitation on the application of this model is the case of Phineas Gage—generally considered "neuroscience's most-celebrated case." Phineas Gage was a railroad foreman in the 1840s who was generally considered a good worker and responsible foreman. One day, as he was tamping gunpowder into a hole, preparing the ground for a blast to create an opening for more rail, the powder ignited. This explosion sent the tamping rod through his left cheek and exiting through the top of Gage's head. A hole of about 1 ½ inches was left at an angle through the left side of his head. Remarkably, Gage was not killed in the accident, and he was even able to go to a doctor for treatment. However, all documentation indicates that Gage's behaviors changed dramatically after the accident; he was no longer able to control emotions and treated others with considerable disrespect. Studies of the case find that, in addition to injury to the neurons associated with cognition, white matter was severely damaged. White matter of the brain is fatty tissue that facilitates transmission of neural activity (Van Horn et al., 2012). His cognitive system was damaged in multiple ways affecting his ability to compensate.

4 Framing Perception With Media

Introduction

As I wrote in *HTB* (2015), different media facilitate different modes of representation, and a medium brings with it different attributes to consider in assessing rhetoric relative to the available modes (Sorapure, 2005). This point also impacts a given medium's ability to affect meaning-making and perception relative to those modes. A video, for example, facilitates more animation than a slide can within a slide show; however, more digital space is needed to access and view a video than to view a slide show. Further, different slide show tools have different capabilities.

The tools available to both composer and audience become part of the multimodal rhetorical situation, and this impacts the model of cognition as well. Much as an audience's biological attributes affect their ability to learn or understand the world, the technology used to design the message affects which modes of representation and stimuli are included and how they are included. If I have access to only pen and paper to convey a message, that limits the design of the message considerably more than if I have access to a word processor like Word and a graphics tool like Photoshop to compose the message. Access to video production tools gives me even more tools to facilitate a persuasive message. The medium or media used to facilitate cognition is included in the model's principles as a framing attribute. I address this attribute of the model in this chapter by offering suggestions to enable the tool's capabilities to become part of the model's dynamic. I also include in-person or face-to-face interaction among communicants, because Social Presence Theory is included in any discussion of technology and communication. Assessment theory helps facilitate this consideration.

Scholarship in Assessing Multimodal Projects

A growing body of scholarship theorizes ways to evaluate and assess multimodal products in writing and technical communication courses. For example, a 2012 issue of *Technical Communication Quarterly* (Odell and Katz, 2012) provides some insight as do articles in *Computers and Composition Online* (e.g.: Murray, Sheets, and Williams, 2010; and Remley, 2010 and 2012). I call attention to some of the points presented in this scholarship about assessing multimodal projects, because it contributes to understanding rhetorical effectiveness of such compositions toward facilitating learning and cognition; but I do not theorize such assessment here.

While some scholars attempt to use design-oriented attributes of rhetoric for assessment, others encourage attributes associated more closely with the reading experience or the learner's cognitive experience. Ball (2006) observes that many rubrics that facilitate assessment of new media projects tend to emphasize attributes of designer skills; she calls for assessment to focus more attention on the rhetoric involved—taking the reader's perspective (p. 394). Odell and Katz (2009), also, encourage an audience-perspective approach. These scholars recognize the impact of the audience's perception of the world and ability to understand a given message.

Certain attributes of rhetoric can apply across modes of representation, as identified by the aforementioned scholars. However, the capabilities and limitations of the media and related tools used to compose the message affect design decisions and, consequently, the rhetoric of the message. The tools to which a composer has access to compose a message and to which an audience has access to view it become part of the rhetorical situation. So, a question I posed in the earlier book and repose here is, does this multimodal product apply effective rhetoric associated with cognition relative to the capabilities of the medium and tools used to create it and neural functions of cognition? I respond to this question within the model by using affordances and constraints of the media of delivery as a framing principle.

Analysis of Affordances and Constraints

Norman (2002) explains that the affordances and constraints of the technology affect how one can use it. According to Norman, affordances are "the perceived and actual properties of the thing...that determine just how the thing could possibly be used" (p. 9). A constraint is something that limits the way in which an artifact can be used; "Affordances suggest the range of possibilities, constraints limit the number of alternatives" (p. 82). While visual cues associated with the tool can suggest the possibilities of use or limits of use, Norman also acknowledges that affordances and constraints may be part of the medium's design but not immediately visible to the user.

I have noted previously that affordances and constraints of a given tool are relative to the user's previous experiences with similar tools or technologies. Norman (2002) emphasizes first-hand experience as he discusses affordances and constraints; however, secondary research and readings based on others' experiences can inform an analysis of affordances and constraints, too. If one has limited experience with a given tool, her understanding of that tool's capabilities and limitations is shaped as she reads about how someone else used that technology.

Previous experience is part of the model; this is associated with an audience's previous experiences with a given concept or tool. However, a designer's own experiences with a given technology frame how he or she uses that tool to design the message. Many new technologies facilitate learning how to use them by incorporating attributes of older, but similar, technologies. As one looks at the interface of the audio recording application Audacity, for example, one experiences the interface of old tape recorders. As one uses a given technology more often, he or she becomes better familiar with its capabilities. That experience can enable the designer to develop better materials with that tool. Until that happens, though, the design will be limited by the designer's understanding of the tool's abilities.

The Rhetoric of Multimodality

I review much of what I presented in *HTB* about multimodal rhetoric here. In the past several years, a focus of study within multimodal theorization has been on various modal combinations and how they affect meaning-making (Gee, 2003; Lemke, 1998 and 1999; Mayer, 2005; Moreno and Mayer, 2000; Richards, 2003; and Whithaus, 2012). Studies pertaining to this analysis seek to understand rhetorical attributes of mixed modes and when and under what conditions certain combinations are most productive (e.g.: Lemke, 1998 and 1999; and Richards 2003). Indeed, several theories of multimodality and this relationship between print-linguistic text and image have been presented, but each seems to have its own difficulties meeting the challenges of theory development thereof.

An example of such a study is that of Moreno and Mayer (2000). Generally, Moreno and Mayer found that certain combinations of visuals and text information affect learning, suggesting a relationship between modes used to communicate and their rhetorical impact. Relative to the rhetoric of instruction, combining visual and verbal/aural modes of representation is more powerful for accomplishing the instructional purpose than using only narration or visuals alone. From these experiments they formulated several principles associated with multimedia instruction. Mayer (2001) summarizes their multimodal principle with the statement that people learn better when pictures and words are integrated into an instructional message than when only words are used (p. 63). When only words are used people may attempt to "build a visual model," but they may not attempt to do so. If a picture is provided, people can make the visual connection more readily. Mayer also asserts that it is vital to eliminate extraneous material—words, images, and sounds—from any multimedia message. Such irrelevant information "competes for cognitive resources in working memory," disrupting the learner's ability to organize and retain relevant information (p. 113). Tufte (1990) also makes this point relative to PowerPoint slide shows.

Gee (2003) asserts that how people read and think about a particular thing is determined by their experiences with certain social groups. Experience builds synapses that enable one to understand a concept that is similar to something they have already learned faster than if the concept is not similar to a previously learned topic. However, Vygotsky (1978) also applies this attribute of socially-constructed knowledge to the use of tools to complete an activity (activity theory). One learns to use a given tool based on how they observe others use that tool.

Assessment of the Multimodal

As I mentioned in the opening section of the chapter, some scholars have tried to approach assessment from different perspectives—some from the designer's perspective and others from the audience's perspective. For example, Odell and Katz (2009) call attention to the reader's perspective and needs. Morain and Swarts (2012) and I (2012) separately identify particular elements of information design that can be applied in video and other media as well. These include: what and how much information is visible on a page or screen, the pace at which narration that accompanies any images moves, how information and content are organized and transitioned from one point to the next, and other attributes affecting the ability of the audience to understand a message relative to the message's purpose. Neal (2011) also includes elements of pace and the ability to follow the narration as well as effective transitions (p. 96).

In each of these approaches to assessment of multimodal products there is sensitivity to the audience's needs and what will help the audience respond a certain way to the information. However, a new rubric emerges with almost each scholarly publication on the topic. In reflecting on assessment approaches and rubrics of authors of 10 different chapters in an edited collection, Herrington, Hodgson, and Moran (2009) observed that "assessment criteria were not generic; they were tailored to the nature and goals of each project" (p. 204). I have argued that one of the variables confounding multimodal assessment scholarship is that different media facilitate different modal combinations and designs (2010).

The framing principle of the technology's affordances and constraints considers the diversity of potential media and semiotics with each, integrating a criterion like that quoted by Herrington, Hodgson, and Moran: "employ the affordances (capabilities) of the medium you're using in effective rhetorical ways" (p. 205). Effective rhetoric depends on the purpose of the message and the targeted audiences, as found with the Moreno and Mayer studies relative to instruction and learning. Just as the concept of rhetoric generally begins with an understanding of audience and purpose to facilitate designing a message, this model recognizes the media available for designing a message to facilitate cognition for the purpose of learning.

Technology and the Message

In *HTB* I alluded to several questions one can ask relative to the medium/media selected to convey a message. These were:

a   How well can the tool synthesize a limited number of modes to facilitate a given message?
b   How well can the tool integrate multiple modes simultaneously or asynchronously?
c   How well are two particular modes that facilitate information well in combination integrated using the tool?
d   How well can space be used within the tool? and
e   Can different modes be integrated effectively separately into the design using timing settings?

A synthesis of these items suggests that the ability of the tool to facilitate particular modes associated with a given rhetorical effort and the timing of those modes in combination or separately within the space provided are affected by the tool's affordances and constraints. However, which tools are available are affected by technology present at the time. For example, prior to television, radio was the most far reaching form of public broadcast; one had to consider the lack of a visual mode of representation.

Writing Technologies and New Media

People can create slide shows that integrate audio narration to describe processes or propose changes. Designers create videos, including those that use virtual environments and place them on the Internet via YouTube for the public to find and view. However, these can also appear through links to Web sites. In this section I describe attributes of each medium affecting design and cognition. The specific examples of each medium that I mention to illustrate the problem and related attributes are associated with subsequent chapters.

Video Rhetoric

A medium common to multimodal forms of persuasion is video. Again, the tool's ability to integrate various modes and one's ability to use the tool affect design. iMovie and Movie Maker have their own strengths and weaknesses as video production tools. For example, iMovie allows for more tools to be used for viewing (export media) than Movie Maker; and iMovie is strictly for Mac machines while Movie Maker is for PCs; so the particular operating system one has greatly affects which tool one can use for video production. However, one uses such tools depending on how they understand they can be used. Some have more experience with a given tool than others, and this affects how they design persuasive messages with them.

Multimodal Instructional Theory: Narration/Images

In *HTB* I included a brief section on multimodal instructional theory related to the combination of narration and images. I include a similar section here, but there is an entire chapter on narration and persuasion later in this book.

Relative to instructional design, Mayer (2005) acknowledges the importance of presenting both images and words in conjunction with each other. Such presentation helps the learner "to hold mental representations of both in working memory" (p. 96). According to Baddeley's (1986) model of working memory, there is a phonological (auditory) channel and a "visuo-spatial" (visual) channel associated with short-term memory. Schnotz (2005) suggests that when a visual image is presented to a reader, the reader can create a visual model as he/she listens to a narrative about the picture (pp. 54–55). By facilitating use of both channels, people can better process information than they can when too much of one system is used. However, the quality of the narration may be affected by the tool used to create it. In each case, though, design needs to consider the capabilities of the tool to facilitate certain content and cognition. In the chapter on narration and persuasion, I present examples using video as well as print to illustrate the affordances and constraints of each.

Social Presence and Persuasion

According to Social Presence Theory, social presence is the degree of the quality of "being there" between two communicators using a communication medium. Media have different levels of social presence. Certain media have a higher degree of social presence, or the feeling of being in person with the other communicator. For example, video is generally considered to have high social presence while audio has little social presence. Media that has a high degree of social presence are considered more sociable, warm, and personal than those with low degree of social presence. In video, the viewer can see the speaker's face, facial expressions, tone of voice, and other stimuli that affect perception in much the same way as if the two were present in the same place. Audio alone is like speaking to someone via the telephone; one has to imagine the other's face and does not experience other stimuli that may affect the message.

This theory is important given that persuasion may occur from some distance or in person. However, the delivery mode used is affected by one's ability to "be there." However, if the communicants are in the same place at the same time, it opens the door to several other phenomena that influence perception and persuasion. These can include dress, smell, and the environment generally. I elaborate on this in a later chapter.

Conclusion

Given the impact that a tool's capabilities have on design relative to a given medium, assessment needs to explicitly integrate such consider-ations. Recognizing the differences in the capabilities of different media and different tools helps consider how they may be used to design instruc-tional materials that affect cognition. Part of the rhetorical situation is choosing which medium or media to use to design a message. This decision frames the design of the message itself; consequently, this is an important framing principle of the model.

5   Narrative and Persuasion

Narrative is very much a part of persuasive rhetoric in both a traditional sense and a multimodal sense. Aristotle observes a relationship between narrative and persuasion, albeit very late in his work on the *Art of Rhetoric* (it is discussed only within the last five sections of the entire work); and all the scholarship in neuroscience related to persuasion articulates its value as well. Narrative engages the audience with a way to assimilate with the speaker, and recent research in neuroscience has found that there are neural dynamics at work when an audience experiences any kind of rhetoric. The narrative is likely to link closely with the audience's prior experiences; so, that is where it can be considered within the model.

There are many attributes of a narrative message that activate neural responses; for example, as a speaker compares him or herself with an audience, trying to make themselves seem like a member of the audience, mirror neurons are activated in the audience; the audience wants to be like that person represented in the narrative. Further, if an outcome of value to the audience is part of the narrative, reward neurons may be activated as well. For example, depending on who it is that is providing the narrative or who is being used as the persona of the narrative, it may also elicit reward neurons if that person is esteemed in an audience's perception: "If I am like that person, I will have the same lifestyle and rewards he/she has."

In this chapter I apply the model to analysis of persuasion related to narrative. I do not expound on the full variety of stimuli that generate neural responses that affect an audience's perception of a message. I limit this discussion to three relatively easy attributes that have already been discussed to some degree in rhetoric and writing scholarship.

The primary neuroscientific concepts involved in persuasion that do not explicitly overlap with concepts of rhetoric and to which I will limit discussion in this chapter are the concepts of "mirror neurons," "reward neurons," and "plasticity." However, concepts from rhetoric such as logos, pathos, and ethos as well as social construction of knowledge are closely connected to these concepts, and an evolving corpus of scholarship on multimodal rhetoric informs how to compose effective messages with different media and modes relative to various combinations. For example, researchers have found that certain colors elicit certain neural responses in viewers.

In this chapter I detail scholarship that recognizes the value of narrative within business communication and technical communication settings. I link this scholarship to more recent scholarship related to neuro-marketing, especially. I describe examples of its integration within these messages as well as within proposals for process improvement. Finally, I offer suggestions on how to provide training and instruction of narrative within multimodal persuasive messages.

The Rhetoric of Narrative

Several years ago Blyler and Perkins devoted an entire issue of the *Journal of Business and Technical Communication* to detailing the value of narrative in professional and scientific practice (1999a). They also presented a compilation of works regarding how professionals in business and technical fields use narrative (1999b). Denning (2005) advances their work, calling attention to the use of narrative to move people to action, share values, and build trust. These and other works establish the importance of narrative as a rhetorical mode in workplace practices. According to Blyler and Perkins (1999a), narratives help to "align and consolidate activities" (p. 246) and "are vital to scientific invention and discovery" (p. 248).

Professionals recognize narrative as a powerful rhetorical tool in business writing and technical writing settings. Narrative provides descriptive accounts of events while offering critical reflection to move an audience to action no matter in what persuasive context it is used. It can motivate readers toward certain action in proposals, and it can interest the reader of a resume to be interested in talking more with a job applicant.

Narrative includes precise details of an event that occurred in the past which are reported in the same order in which they occurred, as well as an observation or evaluation of the information by the narrator (Rentz, 1992). This evaluation facilitates action based on the relationship between the events reported and that analysis. Narrative, generally, is distinguished from argument in its concern with the particular instead of with generalizations.

Much scholarship argues the rhetorical value of narrative in professional writing settings (Rodgers, 1989; Rentz, 1992; Blyler, 1995 and 1996; Blyler and Perkins, 1999; Popken, 1999; and Jameson, 2004). Jameson observes that narrative contributes to "a hybrid, internally dialogic language that fulfills a social purpose by reflecting human relationships even when the subject matter is impersonal and technical." Popken argues that resumes serve as a narrative of one's accomplishments and credentials. Indeed, as mentioned above, Blyler and Perkins devoted an entire issue of the *Journal of Business and Technical Communication* and edited a book detailing the value of narrative in professional and scientific practice (1999). In addition to effecting persuasive rhetoric, Blyler asserts that professional narratives can acculturate students to professional writing. Students can learn how to use disciplinary discourse toward becoming part of the professional community. Neurons are involved in that formation and learning process. Consequently, in addition to serving multiple purposes in practice, it can serve several purposes in workplace writing pedagogy as well.

In spite of this scholarship, professional writing pedagogy still seems to undervalue narrative instruction (Beemer, Bowles, and Shaver, 2005). Students need to review existing narratives within persuasive messages and practice developing narratives within specific applications so as to understand their effectiveness. Further, integrating instruction in how neurons respond to narratives within persuasive messages will enhance that learning as well.

The Rhetoric of Narrative in Professional Settings

Blyler, Rentz, Rodgers, and others have argued narrative's value within a variety of genres used in professional and technical writing practices. Professional narratives integrate many of the attributes of personal narrative. While there is less focus on the individual who is writing the piece, the writer must be able to articulate a sequence of events and offer critical reflection about the relationship of those events to some particular issue or concern. While such passages are shorter than those found in composition essays, they perform similar rhetorical functions. Further, professional narratives offer insight into professional discourses. Students exposed to such narratives can learn the discourse of professionals within a given field (Blyler, 1995 and 1996).

A number of the attributes of narrative are useful in proposal writing and other forms of persuasion; these attributes give narrative qualities that meet the appeals of logos, pathos, and ethos. Rentz asserts further that narratives are a form of discourse tool, and Blyler acknowledges that narratives are valuable because they are related to the communities in which we live; as such it has ethnographic qualities about it and social organization is maintained through stories (p. 295).

Indeed, the more one can establish him or herself as a member of the audience's community the better one can persuade the audience to act on a message. This may be through sharing an experience the speaker had that the audience is likely to have had or by posing as a member of that community by wearing clothes members of that community frequently wear. Consider the politician on a campaign trail who visits a local restaurant. He or she is more likely to be wearing informal shirt and pants than a suit more appropriate for the office to which he or she is vying for election. Simons and Jones (2011) note that this is an effort to affect the audience's mirror neurons. The speaker/candidate is mirroring the target audience's appearance (p. 166).

Another attribute important to persuasion is establishing agreement between the speaker and audience to facilitate understanding and action. Pillay (2011) calls this "facilitated consensus." He states that, "an important part of the mirror neuron system (shared emotion) is implicated in the art of persuasion" (p. 79). Pillay and several others (Boudreau, Coulson, and McCubbins, 2011; Dooley, 2012; and Simons and Jones, 2011) note that the ethos of the narrator can also affect neural processes associated with persuasion. Specifically, trust and expertise are very important attributes of ethos that affect the audience's perception of the message, including narration. Klucharev, Smidts, and Fernandez (2008) found that a single viewing of an expert with a given object provided a positive, lasting effect on memory and attitude for the object. Pillay, in particular, notes that expertise may affect reward neurons (p. 79).

Nahai (2012), also, notes how narrative can be used to elicit empathy. The more one knows another's "story" the more they are to sympathize with that person's plight. Legal scholarship has found that "juries often empathize with plaintiffs" (Faff and Sherman, p. 420). Again, the mirror neurons are at work in such instances; the audience comes to understand why the plaintiff did something and consider a similar situation when they were affected similarly though may not have acted upon that feeling.

Practical Applications

Companies can use multimodal persuasive messages in a variety of media and for various audiences—internal and external. Shaw, Brown, and Bromiley (1998) acknowledge 3M's use of narrative in business planning, using it to present "strategic stories" behind items in bullet-point listings. Fleming (2001) acknowledges the importance of organizational leaders being able to assimilate with employees and encourage reform through narratives. He explains sense-making and sense-giving, two important functions of leadership, as "providing the insights and raw materials necessary to reform mindsets and practices essential to the newly emerging opportunities" (paragraph 5). He goes on to explain that, "few tools are as powerful and readily available to the leader as the use of personal and organizational narrative. Learning to listen to, tell and interpret stories within the organization helps leaders to maximize their sensemaking/sensegiving role" (paragraph 7). Such narratives trying to persuade employees toward organizational change can be delivered in writing or video or through live presentations.

One needs only to look at commercials and advertisements on television and the Web to find examples of multimodal persuasive rhetoric for external audiences. I provide three examples to illustrate the neuroscience associated with persuasion. The first example comes from the marketing materials of a particular law firm. The law firm addresses several kinds of legal cases, including personal injury. One of the main purposes of advertisements, of course, is to persuade the viewer/reader to buy or use the advertiser's product or service. However, there is a unique dynamic within the advertisements of this law firm that is very uncommon among such advertising. These attributes and the neuroscience behind them contribute to creating a certain perception of the law firm's ability to represent clients in personal injury cases especially.

The second example is a public service announcement featuring a narrative of a patient whose cancer was caused by smoking cigarettes and who now receives a particularly painful-looking treatment for her cancer. The images of the treatment invoke both mirror and reward neurons in a negative way, eliciting fear. The third example is of a candidate running for a local elected office. His narrative elicits mirror neural activity as he connects with the local population in several ways.

Law Firm Commercial

Jeffrey Friedman, an attorney, is the face of a particular law firm in almost all of its advertisements and commercials; and he is paralyzed from the waist down (Friedman, Domiano, and Smith Co., L.P.A., 2015). In the commercials and advertisements, he sits in a wheelchair; and this is clearly visible to the viewer. In several commercials, in a gentle, sympathetic tone, he talks about his own experience in a car accident that put him in the wheelchair and how he can represent injured clients better than other attorneys could because of that experience. Several attributes of the multimodal experiences in this narrative come together to make for a persuasive message: these include the speaker himself— physical appearance and ethos, the narrative he provides, and the tone of voice he uses (audio).

The visual appearance of this man in a wheelchair immediately elicits empathy and understanding from the viewer, who may be so injured. The visual dominance attribute of the model is apparent, and it is facilitated through the medium; the commercial's ability to show him in the wheelchair positions him in a similar way as potential clients who may be in a wheelchair. This activates mirror neurons, consequently. The visual appearance is facilitated through television; so visual dominance certainly applies. In some of the commercials, the viewer sees Jeffrey's face first, and the camera pans out eventually to show the entire image of him in the wheel chair. So, the slow progression—filtering— allows the viewer to slowly process the image and absorb more information along the way.

Even if one is not injured, one feels a connection to the speaker; because he has some degree of expertise with the situation they may be experiencing—as an attorney specializing in personal injury and as one who actually experienced it. As an attorney trained in personal injury law, of course, he is considered an expert in personal injury law and litigation. Consequently, one knows that he is a credible source for legal knowledge and practice. However, he is also "expert" in the experiences one who has been severely injured physically may have. The effect of this enhances the mirroring dynamic; he has actually experienced the pain and suffering a potential client is experiencing.

The narrative further places him on the same level as anyone who has been injured in any kind of car accident. Depending on how long the commercial is he provides a certain amount of detail. The gist is that he suffered permanent injuries because of a driver's negligence. There is a detailed video and text on the firm's website that more fully explain the accident (Friedman, Domiano, and Smith Co., L.P.A., 2015). The medium also facilitates the temporal synchronicity and modal filtering attributes of the model. The viewer hears his story at the same time that he or she sees his condition as wheelchair-bound. Further, we hear his message and its tone while watching the expressions on his face. Both are empathetic, not just sympathetic. These further activate mirror neurons; he understands the condition others who are injured are in.

The narrative provided on that webpage featuring his story includes introductory text describing his character: "When you meet Jeff in person, you experience first-hand his kind, hardworking, and genuine character. However, not everyone knows about his lifelong physical battles and how one car accident changed his life and enriched his spirit to become the successful human being and lawyer he is today" (paragraph 1). It goes on to describe details of the night on which the crash occurred: "The driver lost control of the vehicle and veered off the road. He crashed the car into one tree and then another" (paragraph 2). It also includes information about his undergraduate education, professional training, and academic and professional successes. The last paragraph of the narrative about the law firm and his story includes the statement, "When Jeff says to his clients, 'I know, I've been there,' it's the truth. He is the real deal" (paragraph 10).

Again, this activates mirror neurons by helping the viewer understand details of his situation and the accident that paralyzed him. It also enhances his credibility as one who understands his clients who have experienced such a car accident and injury. He shares the same story they may have experienced. The last statement I note above explicitly places him in a common community with potential personal injury clients.

Finally, in commercials and the video on the webpage about his story he uses a calm, sympathetic voice as he talks about his story and the firm. Imagine the difference between being yelled at because you were in a car accident and someone comforting you with a gentle, sympathetic, even empathetic, voice. One is naturally drawn to the sympathetic voice.

This makes using his firm more appealing an option, too. The perception is that he understands his clients' needs and feelings more than a typical personal injury attorney can.

The goal of personal injury litigation is some form of financial compensation to assist with life expenses, health care, and "pain and suffering" directly associated with the injury. The narrative includes information about the firm's successful litigation and specific awards for clients. The webpage also includes video testimonials from satisfied clients. These could activate reward neurons, because the viewer would begin to understand how much compensation he or she could receive by using the law firm to represent them. This is also part of the neural plasticity dynamics of the audience the message targets; the general American public is very interested in financial rewards, especially the potential of winning hundreds of thousands, if not millions, of dollars from litigation. When we read in the newspaper or on television or the Internet of such awards given to those who were injured, it becomes part of our culture. Consequently, prior experience associated with reading or learning of such rewards is relevant as well. As mentioned above, neural plasticity facilitates learning of one's culture and how one understands the world. It shapes their understanding of reality.

If the firm is as successful representing the prospective client as it has been with others, they stand to gain a large amount of compensation. Recall that reward neurons are stimulated by the prospect of a reward, not by actually receiving the award; and they are part of the system that motivates one toward action. So, between appearing as a member of the same community as one who is injured, thereby understanding their needs better than other attorneys, and demonstrated successful litigation, based on previous successes, the advertisement is very persuasive. A viewer would perceive that they could be represented by one who not only has their interests in mind, but empathizes with them; and the viewer may understand the likelihood of receiving a large financial reward given the firm's previous success.

Before moving to the next illustration, I want to point out that another attorney has integrated a similar kind of narrative into his law firm's advertising. Tom Merriman calls attention to the empathy he is able to feel for personal injury clients by explicitly noting that "money was the last thing on my mind" when his daughter was hit by a car (Landskroner Grieco Merriman, LLC, 2015). This statement is similar to Friedman's narrative about his own injury. It places Merriman in the same community as one who may have an injured relative.

Public Service Announcement: Anti-smoking Campaign

Various entities can produce advertisements that attempt to change the way one thinks about a particular phenomenon, activity or policy.

Generally, these are prominent in political debates around election season. I discuss a certain kind of public service announcement in another chapter, because it pertains more to a different attribute than narrative. The example I provide in this chapter focuses on narrative as a persuasive strategy. However, unlike the Friedman narrative, it is used to invoke fear in the viewer.

The Centers for Disease Control and Prevention (CDC) produces a series of commercials/public service announcements known as "Tips From Former Smokers™" that target smokers or those considering smoking toward discouraging such activity. The narratives call attention not only to possible health consequences, but also to the indignities and pain related to treatments associated with those effects. In each commercial a former smoker shares their own narrative about the connection between the particular ailment and smoking, and then they talk about the treatment they receive for it.

One such narrative is that of Marlene, a 68-year old woman who began smoking in high school and now suffers macular degeneration related to her smoking. She talks about this background in the particular commercial. She receives medication for her condition via a shot in her eye, and she describes this experience. The announcement appears in both print and television. Both feature images of her preparing to receive a shot in the eye with an image of the needle in the background. This, of course, applies the attribute of visual dominance, but it does so in a way different from that of the law firm commercial. It focuses on fear and pain—eliciting fear in the amygdala. The amygdala wants to preserve the person, and the hippocampus will help the viewer recall memories of shots and pokes in the eye that were painful. This is all re-enforced through the visual images the viewer sees. The print ad (Figure 5.1) represents this image as she is about to receive the shot.

As with the law firm commercial, television also facilitates temporal synchronicity, intermodal redundancy, and modal filtering. We hear Marlene's story as we see her experiencing treatment. The visual image of her receiving the shot in the eye filters the viewer's focus to that particular experience. She encourages the viewer not to end up like her because, "it's horrible."

This narrative also engages mirror neurons as well as reward neurons, though in very different ways than the previous example. The commercial applies several concepts from the model as well. Again, visual dominance, prior experience, and intermodal redundancy are prominent. The viewer sees her experience with the treatment, and most people would understand the pain associated with any shot from their own experiences. Some may understand what it is like to be poked in the eye; so, the viewer is especially empathetic as we see her receive the shot. Visually and through audio narration the message is re-enforced; so, multiple modes are used to effect a response.

Figure 5.1 Marlene Advertisement. Courtesy of the Centers for Disease Control and Prevention (CDC), 2015 Tips From Former Smokers™ campaign.

The viewer does not want to end up like her; we do not want to mirror that experience and experience the consequence associated with that particular eye disease which may be caused by smoking. So, mirror neurons and reward neurons are engaged in a negative way.

Narrative and Political Campaign Rhetoric

Political campaigns include not only information about the candidates' policy positons but also information about the candidates' background—their personal narratives. This information helps to position the candidate on a similar level with his or her constituents. Much like the law firm's advertising described above, this helps make the candidate seem like one who can empathize with the audience to which he or she is trying to appeal. There is an appeal to mirror neurons. Further, images used in such advertising may re-enforce that connection.

If the candidate is vying for a local political office, the candidate attempts to show the voters his or her connection to the people of that district or city. I describe here a political campaign flyer I received from a candidate for local mayoral office, specifically the narrative it offers coupled with the image provided.

The candidate distributed flyers across the city, and this flyer emphasized the candidate's citizenship and experience in another elected office—the local school board—and lifelong connection with the city.

These attributes make for a narrative emphasizing connection with the community. Further, a photograph of the candidate and his family re-enforce this connection. I provide specific detail of each.

In the flyer the particular candidate lists that he graduated from the local school district and that he married someone from the city, listing his wife's name and including her maiden name. This is important, because her family is prominent in the city. By stating her last name, the candidate appeals to "lifers;" those who have lived in the city all their life. This would stimulate mirror neurons in an audience, helping them identify with the candidate as one of them, having knowledge of the city's history, and being concerned about how to advance the city. The candidate also acknowledges his position on the local school board, showing investment in the community and listing his leadership experience as school board president for several years.

The candidate includes a picture of himself, dressed professionally; his wife and their son, both dressed in a sporty look. The picture appears to be outside their home. His wife, in addition to being from a prominent local family, is a teacher in the local school district; and some citizens may have had or have a child with her as their teacher. Including her in the photo helps them make a connection to their own children's future. The visual image facilitates that connection through the Colavita visual dominance effect. Their son was a student in the local district; so, some people may know of him as well. If he is generally recognized as a good student or good person, seeing him in the flyer further appeals to the audience.

The photograph of the family does several things to stimulate neural processes. Showing the family as one, it stimulates mirror neurons; the audience wants the city to act as a unit like a family. Having the family dress nicely further stimulates mirror neurons; the community in general is recognized as "middle class America," and the family is represented as such. So, the dress stimulates mirror neurons, re-enforcing the candidate's connection with the community in general and its identity.

The flyer uses multiple modes (images and print) to re-enforce the candidate's connection with the community—intermodal redundancy. The candidate also mentions several places/activities where people may have met or interacted with him—prior experiences. The flyer uses multiple modes (images and print) to re-enforce the candidate's connection with the community—intermodal redundancy. The candidate also mentions several places/activities where people may have met or interacted with him—prior experiences.

Temporal synchronicity and modal redundancy come into play when considering the positioning of the text and image of him and his family. The visual image is shown alongside the text listing his accomplishments. So, the reader sees his image with his family as well as his accomplishments relatively close in proximity and time as he or she reviews the flyer.

The photograph of the family does several things to stimulate neural processes. Showing the family as one, it stimulates mirror neurons; the audience wants the city to act as a unit like a family. Having the family dress nicely further stimulates mirror neurons; the community in general is recognized as "middle class America," and the family is represented as such. Again, the balance between picture and print-linguistic text shows connections between the model's attributes in influencing perception.

Conclusion

These descriptions of particular multimodal persuasive messages and neural dynamics associated with them provide an illustration of the kinds of practical applications students and practitioners alike can review to improve their understanding of persuasive narratives.

6 Dress and Natural [Neural] Codes
Smell, Setting, and Audience

When you watch political campaign commercials or see political advertisements that include the candidate or politician, do you notice how candidates will appear wearing various kinds of dress depending on their message and setting for the commercial? Generally, if one is shown in a local restaurant dining with citizens of that locale, the candidate is dressed down—wearing a polo shirt and jeans or something only a little sporty. The general message when they do that is that they are like the members of that community and, as such, can represent those people well. Consider the effect this has on audiences.

Further, consider the impact of a message if you have actually attended a political campaign event or policy introduction. Being in the same place as the speaker and experiencing the atmosphere of the moment combined with the verbal and visual messages to elicit certain responses one may not have if viewing it on television. So, a physical proximity between speaker and audience contributed to the rhetorical effect. Generally, when one considers "medium" the term is defined as a form of technology—personal or broadcast; print, video, computer-mediated communication in various forms. I argue in this chapter that in-person or face-to-face communication be considered within the discussion of medium used for communication, especially relative to persuasive communication because the context of face-to-face, same proximity enables additional modes of representation to impact the message.

In this chapter I describe the effects of non-verbal attributes of the message further—dress, context/environment, and how real-time, same location dynamics affect the message and its neuro-rhetoric. I also expound on the sense of smell and its relationship to multimodal persuasive messages and the model.

Dress

As I mentioned in the previous chapter, studies have shown that people are attracted to others with whom they assimilate; people who are like them in some way. Political advertisers understand this and try to integrate certain dress in certain messages. If the politician is speaking about education policy, they may wear a professional dress, as teachers may dress. If the appeal is directed at the general public, their dress may be less formal. If the message pertains to business policy, they will dress as business professionals. However, assimilation is effective with certain messages but not others. In some cases the audience is persuaded by someone who is not like them but represents some expertise they lack but recognize as valuable to them for a particular situation—such as the attorney's expertise with litigation when considering a lawsuit.

If someone dressed as a doctor tells the general public that smoking is bad for their health it carries more persuasive weight than if someone dressed casually—perhaps looking like a member of the general public—makes the same statement. The difference is that the person dressed as a doctor is representing him or herself as a member of a community that has expertise in healthy lifestyles, while the other speaker is not. The audience would find the statement more valuable coming from the health expert. What if the doctor were not dressed as a doctor but as a member of the general public? He or she would need to make a statement about their status as a doctor in order for the message to have the same effect.

Much of the dress code-related rhetoric is derived from the dynamics of neural plasticity—how neurons develop and react to certain stimuli over time. It is through conversations and experience that people learn to react certain ways to others and some stimuli, including dress. If I grow up in a small community where no one wears formal outfits, even to work at local stores, I may not understand what to do or how to react when someone wearing a suit come to my town. As such the mere wearing of the suit invokes fear in me, and I perceive the person as someone I need to avoid.

I present an example of how dress and plasticity could affect the rhetoric in a classroom setting. As such the notion of social presence, described briefly in Chapter 4, is the highest it can be; while various media facilitate some degree of social presence face-to-face contact with someone in the same physical proximity not facilitated via any form of technology is recognized as the highest level of social presence. So, the rhetoric is somewhat affected by that heightened social presence.

In a classroom setting, there may be a group of students who are often disruptive, talking in class while the professor is lecturing or showing an illustration of something; and they respond differently to approaches from the professor to quiet them. If another student quieted them, a number of attributes of neuroscientific dynamics and multimodal persuasion may be at play, and I discuss each.

Pretend that a small group of disruptive students sits together at one of the main corners of the class room. They often talk amongst themselves, usually about class-related topics but sometimes about other topics. Some of these are loud enough for all of the students to hear. When the conversation gets to that level, the professor, like many instructors would probably do, generally gives them a look or short reminder to quiet down, letting them know they were loud and disrupting class to some degree, and to persuade them to tone their conversation down so as not to disturb other students' learning. When the professor gives the look, they quiet down for the rest of the class period; but the same disruptions occur throughout the semester. Indeed, this happens more than a handful of times during the course of the semester.

Professors wear various styles of dress. Some often dress casually while others usually wear professional clothes; a male, for example, may wear a dress shirt, tie and suit or sport coat and dress pants along with dark socks and dress shoes. One may assume that students would respect the instructor's position, and clothing could re-enforce that position as well as model professionalism. It would be troubling to most professors that this group of students would repeat the disruptive behavior in spite of the professor having warned them on a few occasions. Perhaps they just did not realize that they were talking as loudly as they were, or, perhaps, they did not care. Nevertheless, the other students seem to understand the effort to quiet the group, but the disruptive group persists with their disruptive behavior anyway. What happens when different people in that classroom attempt to quiet the disruptive group?

In one particular class period near the end of the semester, the group becomes loud again. One student, male or female, gets up when the group becomes loud, walks over to the group and says in an assertive voice, "I'm trying to learn. Please be quiet." The group seems to react to their message immediately and are quiet the rest of the semester.

The message is, in essence, the same as that offered by the professor; "Please be quiet so other students can hear what I'm saying and can learn." Yet, it isn't the professor who makes the statement. While it occurred briefly and explicitly, several dynamics may be at work in this example, depending on the student's gender and dress, among other attributes. Most students respect authority and will pay attention to their teacher, recognizing the teacher as holding a position of authority within the classroom. However, there are students who have trouble with authority figures and exhibit rebellious behavior as a means to counter authority. Most students respond to authority, but some do not. Such students may not care who the authority figure is. Some students respond to actions of peers with more respect than they do to the actions of other adults. It may be that the group was shocked that one of their own peers would challenge their behavior and that they understood that this person represented others in the class. Their mirror neurons were challenged with regard to what they expected of their peers. They expected, perhaps, that their classmates were okay with them challenging the professor's authority; and, until a classmate told them otherwise, they continued.

As a student, the one who confronted the group may be wearing an outfit typical of any college student. That would further engage mirror neurons of those in the disruptive group, re-enforcing that the challenger is a peer. Again, this may contribute to their confusion and their being startled by the student's action. The student may dress nicely, beyond the normal casual or sporty-casual wear most students usually wear. This does not change the mirror dynamic much, because any student may dress just as nicely at any given time during the semester. What if the student dresses in an unusual way? That may change the mirror dynamics and affect other dynamics as well.

Some students participate in leadership training programs (a business leadership program or Reserve Officer Training Corps (ROTC), for example) and occasionally wear clothing related to that training to class—a business suit, for example. ROTC provides tuition assistance; so, a student may use the program as a form of financial aid. In this example, pretend that the student was participating in an ROTC program and wore their ROTC officer outfit to class the day the incident happened. Now, not only does the peer dynamic affect the reaction of the group, but dress may affect it as well.

The dress uniform may affect the rhetoric in this situation, because the ROTC dress uniform may be perceived not only as "official" but, also, as intimidating. It is a military outfit, representing defense and aggressive action. Given the general fear most people have when involved in an aggressive encounter, dynamics related to the amygdala and hippocampus are involved.

Again, the amygdala is concerned with basic needs, including survival, and reacts with fear to any situation it does not know how to manage. Further, the hippocampus helps recall memories so that we understand how we reacted to a given situation in the past; however, if that situation was a negative experience, we recall that negativity.

Finally, the student's leadership training in the ROTC program would contribute to their comfort with taking a stand in this case. Whether male or female, the student may have acted more assertively than they otherwise would have because they were addressing peers and felt confident in their ability to manage the situation. They may not have realized that their uniform contributed to the rhetorical impact the entire encounter had; nevertheless, the combination had the desired effect.

These dynamics would have engaged mirror neurons as well as amygdala/hippocampus, as stated above, more than any other neural activity. Several attributes of the model can be applied. However, it introduces another phenomenon to the model's concept of medium used and how it may affect other attributes of the model—physical proximity. Connection to prior experience has been mentioned already; that the message occurred in the same location as the audience could affect intermodal redundancy, temporal synchronicity, modal filtering and visual dominance.

Real-time, Same Proximity as Medium

Technology can serve as a buffer between speaker and audience; as such the audience feels safe even when threatened. One cannot possibly hurt me through television, computer, telephone, or any other medium; because they cannot immediately touch me and I can change my interaction with it. However, when the speaker is face-to-face with the audience, as may happen in an office setting or classroom or public place, the message may have a very different impact just because of that proximity. This is part of the medium used to facilitate communication, and it facilitates additional modes of representation such as smell and feel, which are not possible to include in a digital medium or print.

I alluded to the concept of social presence before; how technology can create the perception of close physical proximity between communicants. The more visual and real-time interaction the technology can facilitate, the higher the level of social presence. Face-to-face is considered the highest level of social presence; so, if the speaker and audience are in the same physical location at the time the message is presented, it is the highest level of social presence. Generally, studies find that there is a greater response to persuasive messages within higher social presence contexts; so, it is relevant to include it among the dynamics affecting persuasion. In a situation in which one wants to persuade a single person or small group, it is likely most effective to do it in-person.

The audience experiences intermodal redundancy of the speech as well as dress and facial expression of the speaker. The visual experience is immediate and real; the audience sees the person in its presence. Further, the temporal synchronicity of the message—and response—is immediate. Consequently, this illustrates the effect that changing the medium has on the other attributes of the model. The audience also experiences the smells of the setting, be it an outdoor space that includes floral scents or an inner-city space that includes industrial smells.

Further, the touch of a speaker may contribute to his or her rhetoric. One may provide a condolence message via letter or e-mail, but the message is different when the speaker offers a calming touch of the shoulder or hug, which can only occur in-person. Even the threat of touch, as in the example described above, could impact a message more persuasively than if the message had been conveyed via video.

In a professional setting, consider the role of the presentation or meeting whether a written report accompanies it or not. Proposals that include a presentation allow for interactivity among the communicants as well as additional sensory experiences. A presentation from an attractive person may be received better than one delivered by an unattractive person. A presentation delivered from an attractive person wearing a nice-smelling fragrance—perfume or cologne—may be better received than one from someone who is not wearing cologne or perfume.

Studies have found that even if the environment includes a nice floral smell, it elicits a certain kind of action on the part of the audience. Several studies, in fact, have found that customers are more likely to purchase items in a store that includes floral smells. Cartwright (2014) reported that, "Nike discovered that they could increase the intent to purchase by 80% through the introduction of scent into their stores. Another survey at a petrol station with a mini-mart reported that the aroma of coffee helped boost sales of the beverage by a whopping 300%" (paragraph 7). He also notes that, according to another study by the Smell & Taste Research Foundation, "[m]any of the subjects in the study reported that they were willing to pay $10 more for Nike sneakers placed in scented rooms, than those placed in an unscented one" (paragraph 10).

Floral scents elicit pleasant memories and images in our mind. The hippocampus is involved with memory; and it stores several attributes of experiences, including odors associated with experiences. One may associate a certain smell with an unpleasant experience, and he or she will recall that experience and related feelings about when they encounter that smell.

Smell can be associated with a given product as well. One needs only to review a fashion magazine—men's or women's fashion—to experience marketers' efforts to use scent to engage an audience with a product. Fashion magazines are loaded with advertisements of fragrances that include the scent of the product. Oftentimes, an attractive model accompanies the advertisement as well. This combines the smell and appearance (visual) effects associated with the model. One's hippocampus may be activated by the scent while mirror neurons or reward neurons are activated by the model, depending on the product's target audience. These tactics are involved in face-to-face settings when fragrance models attend store functions that include fragrance sales. Visitors to department stores sometimes encounter a model who appears to be squirting anyone who passes with a perfume or fragrance she is holding. Again, the effect carries over into that encounter and may even include the other stimuli associated with the store or people with the shopper.

The Combined, Multimodal Influence

Much as the combination of the uniform worn by the student and perceptions of her race in the example mentioned above could evoke fear or the perception of aggression, floral scents and attractive people can evoke comfortable feelings and a sense of easiness. Such feelings would be influenced by a combination of neural dynamics involving all the neural items already mentioned—amygdala, hippocampus, reward neurons, and mirror neurons, as was described with that previous example of dress.

Given the literature, one would expect that a presentation given by an attractive person wearing a pleasant fragrance—perfume or cologne—dressed nicely/appropriately for the audience (professional dress for a business meeting, for example; or sporty looking shirt and pants if among the general population) in an outdoor setting or lightly fragrant room and engaging the audience with a friendly face and voice would make for a most-persuasive message almost no matter the message or audience's perception of the issue. There is a certain intoxication about the combination of these attributes in an in-person/face-to-face setting. Consider the neural dynamics at play.

If one is at ease, the amygdala has little to worry about, as its main function is survival. Fewer alarm systems are at work, consequently. The combination also sets the hippocampus at ease, because the audience's memories linked to attractive people, pleasant smells, and friendly interaction, as well as dress that is neither intimidating nor subordinate are generally pleasant. Further, mirror neurons engage if the speaker and audience are the same gender, since the audience wants to consider itself as also attractive and pleasant. If the audience is a different gender than the speaker, reward neurons may be stimulated by the perception of potential or anticipated sexual relations with that person. As such the audience is likely to be more agreeable to a message conveyed by that person than if the speaker were unattractive or had a bad odor about them.

7 Persuasion of Change

Because of its nature, persuasion is generally associated with an effort to change an audience's mind about something. In the field of rhetoric, persuasion and argument are not the same thing; while both are doing similar things, argument suggests a message that is a bit more powerful than general persuasion. Argument suggests there is an active debate about an issue, and the counterarguments are built into an argument in an effort to address both positions while making a case as to which position is the better. I allude to this distinction because in many political advertisements that persuade toward changing society's attitude about a given issue, a counterargument may be presented. However, it is done so, oftentimes, satirically or represented in the advertisement or commercial in a negative light. That is, it is not represented as a serious position.

The previous chapters have shown how particular attributes of a multimodal message can affect its meaning and impact relative to neurobiological phenomena. While I touched on certain attributes of the model in those chapters, I provide considerably more detailed analyses of multimodal persuasive messages in this chapter. In this chapter I provide analysis of commercials pertaining to a specific issue of political concern from 2013–2016—fracking. Fracking involves oil and other energy companies drilling wells that move along an angled hole, not a straight vertical hole, to get to oil and other fuel resources, then using hydraulic means to extract the fuel resources. Because some of the line is horizontal, an outside mechanism is required to move the gas out of the well. The debate, generally, revolves around how safe fracking is to the environment; some have linked fracking to unstable ground contributing to earthquakes, and others have argued that it contributes to contamination of the ground and is also very expensive because of the large amounts of water that must be transported to assist in the process.

I draw, specifically, on efforts in Colorado to enact laws concerning fracking. The three commercials that I draw upon all favor fracking and were produced by different organizations. Two commercials are testimonials by people who are depicted as environmentally conscious supporting fracking as a safe way to access resources. One is a radio advertisement in which the Colorado governor offers testimony about

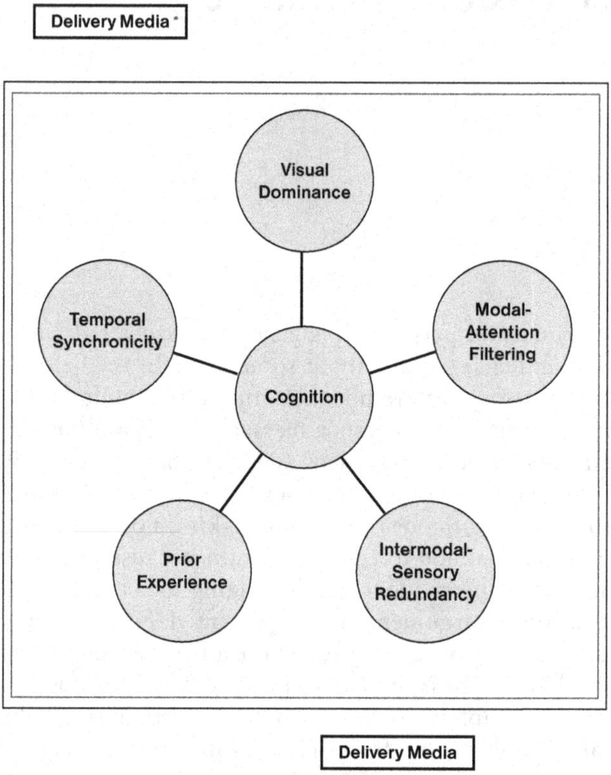

Delivery Media *

Visual Dominance

Temporal Synchronicity

Modal-Attention Filtering

Cognition

Prior Experience

Intermodal-Sensory Redundancy

Delivery Media

Figure 7.1 Model.

fracking laws and safety. Each integrates attributes of neuroscience that I have presented earlier. They appeal to mirror neurons, reward neurons, and elicit reactions from the amygdala and hippocampus as they try to persuade the viewer to allow fracking.

As a reminder of the components of the model, I include it below as Figure 7.1.

Fracking Commercial One Description

The primary commercial I use is a 30-second piece that includes images of a woman, identified by name and state association with print linguistic text as someone from Colorado, who claims to be an outdoor lover, walking through a mountainous landscape with a dog on a sunny day (Energy from Shale, 2015a). She is dressed for the walk wearing khaki pants, a long sporty shirt, and warm vest and boots. She carries a backpack as well. She walks along a mountain pathway and looks at tall trees, and she states in a voice-over narrative that she is "not a big city person. I grew up here. These are my streets; these are my skyscrapers." She and the dog pass three other people; and they acknowledge each other with a friendly wave and smile but do not stop to talk, suggesting they are not familiar with each other. She explains that she is a geologist and works in the energy business, because she understands that fracking is part of energy's future and she wants to make sure there is a balance between fracking activities and the environment's protection. She reassures the viewer that fracking has been occurring safely for over 60 years. The commercial ends with another voice over, male, encouraging the viewer to learn more by going to a particular website while the screen shows text stating "Shale. The energy to do it right" in the center of the screen and textual information about who sponsored the commercial in small print near the bottom of the screen.

Neural Attributes Affecting Rhetoric

Medium—Visual Dominance

The commercial appears on television; so, visual imagery is used throughout, and several visual cues stimulate various neural dynamics that all contribute to the positive message being conveyed. While some text appears and narration is heard, the most dominant mode is the visual. The images associated with the spokesperson, which I describe next; the images of the surrounding setting, and even the inclusion of the image of the dog, all appeal to certain neural dynamics and other attributes of the model.

Primary Spokesperson—Female

The female figure is principally associated with the Prior Experience attribute of the model; however, she also acts in conjunction with other items in the commercial to integrate other attributes of the model as well. She appeals to the hippocampus-placed memories and cultural perception of a mother as a caring person. Women in American culture are generally perceived as nurturing and caring; so, using a woman appeals to that memory and conditioning. This also alleviates any fears a viewer may have about fracking, because the amygdala is satisfied that this person does not represent a danger.

Further, her general appearance is not one that would elicit fear; while not displaying the general "beauty" of a professional model, she is not unattractive. She walks slowly through the terrain, suggesting enjoyment of the experience and appreciation for the environment. Her facial expression, when she speaks directly to the viewer about her career and desire for balance between fracking and nature, is of concern. The amygdala would not announce fear to the viewer.

The clothing she wears can be perceived either as professional or as casual; as a geologist, she spends much time outdoors carrying a back-pack of tools of her trade. However, she may also represent someone on a casual nature hike, because such a person would dress similarly. This is re-enforced by the people she passes; they are dressed similarly but no mention of their career is made. They could easily be anyone who loves nature. As such, mirror neurons are stimulated; the viewer could easily be her.

She states that she is a geologist who works for the energy industry. This positions her as an expert in the field. Consequently, mirror neurons are engaged; while the viewer may not be an expert, the viewer values the expert's testimony, and we want to be like her, striking a balance between nature and use of energy sources.

So, the spokesperson for the particular commercial, representing the energy industry, is also a representative of a caring, nurturing cultural image, and her facial expressions re-enforce that perception and her interaction with other people also re-enforces friendliness. These may trigger mirror neurons in the viewer as well; those who oppose fracking represent themselves as caring about nature.

Narrative—Voice Over

As she talks to the viewer about her background and concern for nature, she uses a comforting tone; one might easily consider it a voice of re-assuring concern, as if to say, "I'm concerned about it, too; and it's okay." The voice-facial expression combination considers the Inter-modal Redundancy attribute as well as Temporal Synchronicity; the narrative, tone and facial expressions re-enforce each other and they are provided at the same time.

Setting—Outdoors

The images shown are of the outdoors, eliciting hippocampus memories of the viewers' own relationship with the outdoors. Generally, we associate freedom, relaxation, and certain smells with the outdoors, especially natural, floral smells with the images shown. There is no image of "the big city" or even of oil drilling equipment. Such an image, of drilling equipment, could be perceived negatively because we generally link the image of an oil well to the messy images of oil slicks or spewing oil. So, the omission eliminates that potential perception while re-enforcing the positive perceptions of the outdoors. Again, these images are part of our memories; so, they would be connected to appeals to the hippocampus. These engage prior Experience as well as Modal Filtering; excluding the image of an oil rig helps to process only positive images.

Inclusion of the Dog

Why would a dog be relevant in a commercial about energy sources? A few responses are valid. There is a certain appeal to nature even when we consider a domesticated animal. So, the dog could represent the balance she speaks of with nature. However, more likely, the dog is included because studies generally find viewers equate a more positive perception of a product or issue when a dog or cat is included in the commercial. This is linked principally to hippocampus memories. Most people have had pleasant experiences with domesticated animals. They are "cute" and "cuddly." Certain breeds of dogs are also considered "loyal" and "friendly," while others may be considered aggressive or threatening such as a Rottweiler, Bulldog, or German Shepherd. The particular breed used in the commercial is not one that would be considered threatening generally. So, the use of the dog has less to do with the issue itself and more to do with an effort to find a way to create a positive perception of the issue. So, again, this item is included within the Prior Experience attribute.

Message—Safe For Over 60 Years

The statement that fracking activity has been going on for over 60 years elicits further appeal to reward neurons and the amygdala. The viewer may not be aware that fracking is not new, and it has been done safely for a long time. So, one could perceive that additional fracking will contribute to rewards—such as lower costs associated with oil products and increased jobs. That is has been done safely for so long also addresses any perceived danger the amygdala may perceive.

People understand that even though they may just be learning about a given phenomenon, if it has already existed and has been proven to be safe, we are reassured of its safety and feel better about it. Through experiences with such events and understanding that they may be new to us but not new generally, we are reassured. So, this also is part of Prior Experience.

Fracking Commercial Two Description

The second commercial is similar to the one I just described. It is a 30-second piece in which a woman narrates how her family allowed companies to build fracking rigs on their ranch after doing some research on its safety and benefits to the economy (Energy from Shale, 2015b). She explains that the ranch has been in the family for a long time; her husband's grandparents built the ranch and they are working hard to maintain it and keep it in good condition. She acknowledges that her family was concerned about fracking and talked to many people "about the facts." She indicates that they found out that fracking is "safe for our land, our water, and the air."

Throughout the commercial images of people working on the ranch are shown at various times of the day and include images of horses, cattle, and a child of approximately 5 years old. In fact, the commercial ends with an image of the couple, a horse, and the child mingling together at sunset as the commercial's sponsor is shown and a voice over encourages the viewer to "get the facts." Further, gentle, comforting music is played throughout.

Because this commercial is very similar to the first, I use many of the same attributes to discuss its relationship to the model.

Neural Attributes Affecting Rhetoric

Medium—Visual Dominance

Like the first, the commercial appears on television; so, visual imagery is used throughout, and the several visual cues stimulate neural dynamics that contribute to the positive message. The images associated with the spokesperson, the images of the surrounding setting, and even the inclusion of the horses and child, all appeal to certain neural dynamics.

Primary Spokesperson—Female

Again, the primary spokesperson is a female, prompting consideration of the Prior Experience attribute of the model. She appeals to memories and cultural perception of a mother as a caring person, alleviating fears a viewer may have about fracking; the amygdala is not alarmed by his person.

Her general appearance also does not elicit fear; as with the first, while she does not display the "beauty" of a professional model, she is not unattractive. Her facial expression, when she speaks directly to the viewer about her family, the ranch, and desire for balance between fracking and maintenance of the ranch, is not one of concern, but reassurance.

The clothing she wears can be perceived as farming or ranch wear. She spends much time outdoors performing various responsibilities on the ranch. This is, also, re-enforced by the other people shown in the commercial— likely her family. They are dressed similarly. They could easily be anyone who loves nature and is concerned about their homestead. As such, mirror neurons are stimulated; the viewer could easily be her and her family.

She explains that she was concerned about letting energy companies drill on her ranch and how she was reassured that it was safe after doing some research. Unlike the first commercial, she is not an expert; yet, she is a concerned landowner who has a family that works the land. Consequently, mirror neurons are stimulated; anyone could be like her or someone else in her family.

So, the spokesperson for the particular commercial is representative of a caring, nurturing, cultural image, and her facial expressions re-enforce that perception and her interaction with other people also re-enforces friendliness. These may trigger mirror neurons in the viewer as well; those who oppose fracking represent themselves as caring about nature.

Narrative—Voice Over

As with the first commercial, she talks to the viewer about her background and concern for nature in a comforting tone; one might easily consider it a voice of reassuring concern, as if to say, "I'm concerned about it, too; and it's okay." The voice-facial expression combination considers the Inter-modal Sensory Redundancy attribute as well as Temporal Synchronicity; the narrative, tone and facial expressions re-enforce each other and they are provided at the same time.

Setting—Outdoors

The images shown are of the outdoors, eliciting hippocampus memories of the viewers' own relationship with the outdoors. Unlike the first, though, there is an image of an oil drilling rig, shown for less than two seconds and in the background, the upper left corner of the screen, and taking up about 1/12 of the total space of the screen. An image of drilling equipment could be perceived negatively, but minimizing its appearance helps to filter the information we process. These engage prior Experience as well as Modal Filtering.

Inclusion of Horses and Child

The horse, like the dog in the previous commercial, elicits a warm, fuzzy feeling from the viewer. Again, there is a link to hippocampus memories. This item is included within the Prior Experience attribute.

Studies have also found that including a child, especially an infant, in an advertisement elicits positive perceptions of the product being advertised. Young children are generally perceived as harmless and helpless, needing others to care for them. The viewer lets out an expression of "awwww." The child here, though, also represents the future; the family's future on the ranch, re-enforced by the image at the end in which the child appears with the horse and parents, as well as humanity's future.

Message—Safe

The statement that fracking is safe for the water, land, and air appeals to the amygdala. That "the facts" point to its safety alleviates any concern about perceived danger from the amygdala. Through experiences with research and factual information, we are reassured. So, this also is part of Prior Experience.

Fracking Commercial Three Description

The third commercial I use is actually a 30-second radio commercial; it is exclusively audio testimony from the governor of Colorado (Colorado Oil and Gas Association, 2015). It is sponsored by an energy-related association in the state. Because it is a radio commercial, there cannot be visual images. Consequently, this message takes on some different attributes than the others to effect neural processes related to persuasion. The advertisement caused some concern, because it is recognized by many as the first time a sitting governor has been used in a testimonial to support a given political initiative.

In the commercial the governor identifies himself and explains that Colorado has passed some of the toughest laws pertaining to fracking to ensure safety. He states that the "conservation community and industry" came together to facilitate such laws, and he acknowledges the link to job creation and environmental protection. He never explicitly asks citizens to vote in favor of fracking activity. The sponsor is identified by a different speaker at the very end of the message.

Primary Spokesperson—Male

Whereas the other two commercials used a female, who could be anyone of the public, as the primary speaker, the primary spokesperson is a male who holds a prominent position of authority. This also integrates the Prior Experience in that the listener recognizes the name and voice of the speaker, which immediately leads him or her to think about the person relative to images he or she has seen of the governor. As a public official, we expect him to have concerns of citizens in mind with any action he supports. So, the amygdala is not alarmed by his statements and the hippocampus may feel assured based on its memories of the governor's other actions as governor.

The Visual Dominance attribute is tricky here, too, because it is a radio commercial. However, again, the listener is imagining the governor as he speaks. So, the mind is drawing upon images it has stored in the hippocampus to help imagine or visualize the speaker.

His general appearance is not at all relevant, because it is a radio commercial; however, the same images that help the listener envision him speaking necessarily include appearance and dress relative to memories of any previous images. Further, he is a leader of the state; so, mirror neurons are stimulated; the listener wants to be valued like him.

Like the second commercial, he is not an expert on energy; however, he is an expert on legislation. Consequently, mirror neurons are stimulated because of this expertise. The listener is assured that he knows what he is talking about when he speaks to the effectiveness of the legislation related to fracking.

Narrative—Voice Over

While the previous two commercials emphasized safety through a tone of concern in the voice over, this message seems to emphasize authoritativeness in the safety message. As a recognized leader, the authoritative tone appeals to mirror neurons because of prior experience with leadership and authoritative messages.

The Intermodal Redundancy attribute is challenged somewhat because it is a radio commercial; but, again, the listener imagines an image. So, there may be implied redundancy in this case.

Message—Safe

As with the other messages, the primary message here is safety; however, it also includes job creation as a selling point. This, of course, elicits reward neurons based on prior experience as well. Historically, job creation leads to more people having disposable income and more money is available in the geographic area. Other businesses benefit and individuals benefit from lower taxes and more retail options. They also have more money to be able to buy nice things. The more jobs that can be created, the better the economy can perform, perhaps leading to reduced taxes and/or more public support of various initiatives from taxes raised from employment within the fracking industry. Someone who is underemployed now or unemployed may perceive hope from the governor's statement about job creation; he or she may be able to get a good-paying job in the industry and improve his or her economic situation. So, the listener equates support for fracking with economic rewards for him or herself, even if they are indirect.

"Help Me Stay Rich Colorado" Series

In many cases, an organization will attempt to use humor and satire in political commercials. There is a series of three particular commercials associated with the effort to allow fracking in Colorado that apply a farcical approach encouraging Coloradoans to help international companies remain wealthy by continuing to use their oil products. One commercial, the longest of the set at two minutes, features a Russian character while the other two feature Middle Eastern characters. I apply a similar analysis to these commercials. All three are sponsored by the same organization, but not the energy industry, as was the case with the other commercials.

Russian Commercial Description (Help Me Colorado, 2014a)

This commercial shows a variety of images of Russia while a wealthy-looking male character, speaking English with a Russian accent, complains that his company and he stand to lose much wealth if Colorado turns to fracking, which would also upset the Russian president. Another male, intimidating-looking, appears in the commercial along with two models in sexy-looking outfits and showing lots of lingerie, using the appeal of sex. There are a total of three unique scenes showing the set of four characters. The first is in the main speaker's very lavish house, the second is on a border with Ukraine and shows the two women holding weapons and dressed in military garb while the other male is dressed as a masked Ninja. The third shows them in front of an imperial-looking building. At different points in the commercial the spokesperson states that Coloradoans finding their own resource "is very disappointing" as he looks into the camera with a stern expression; "Russian energy is the best energy," as he stands in the military scene; and "Independence is not good" in the scene in front of the Imperial building. Finally, near the end he appeals to Coloradoans to "help me stay rich."

Middle Eastern Commercials Description

Two commercials, much shorter in length at less than 20 seconds, show a Middle Eastern male appealing to voters using two different reasons to help him stay rich. In one he appears by himself in front of a strip club and says he needs help employing American women—presumably as strippers (Help Me Colorado, 2014b). In the other (Help Me Colorado, 2014c) he states that he needs to employ several chauffeurs for his wives as he stands in front of two cars and four males dressed as chauffeurs.

Spokesperson—Wealthy International Male

The use of a wealthy foreign persona to appeal to Coloradoans is meant to elicit fear from the amygdala based on prior experiences with news about aggression from those countries against other nations and their wealth related to oil production. The use of a wealthy person, flaunting his wealth would further incite a sort of contrary reward neural reaction; as if to say "why are we rewarding them when we should reward our own economy."

Medium—Television—Visual

In each commercial the male spokesperson is shown wearing a fancy suit while the viewer also sees generally negative images of wealth and corruption. In the first Middle Eastern commercial, an image of a dancing girl is shown behind the man, as a dancing neon light. In the Russian commercial and the second Middle Eastern commercial the male is shown surrounded by images of wealth—cars or fancy home. So, the visual dominance attribute of the model is prominent and elicits several negative perceptions.

Narrative and Message: "Help Me Stay Rich"

The general narrative in all three commercials—I group them because all three attempt the same kind of appeal is that Americans have helped them to become wealthy and they fear losing profits to American companies; so, Americans should feel sorry for them and want to help them retain their wealth. Again there is a negative response from reward neurons such that the implied message of American independence will help America's economy elicits reward neurons for the viewer to support fracking.

Conclusion

The five commercials discussed in this chapter provide evidence of the model's application to multiple versions of the same specific message and in different primary modes. The primary medium used in each facilitates certain attributes of the message and modes used for the message. Even the radio commercial facilitates visualization because it uses a prominent public figure as the speaker, allowing the listener to draw on their memory of what that person looks like.

The model helps us to analyze existing messages to understand particular attributes of them and how they affect neurobiology and perception. The next chapter considers how one may use the model toward producing a persuasive message.

The next set of messages are drawn from the examples I used earlier. While I focused in previous chapters on particular attributes of the advertisements and messages, I detail an analysis related to the model here, calling attention to other attributes.

8   Historical Political Speeches

In this chapter I apply the model to discussion of a few major political speeches that included persuasive rhetoric in some form. All three that I use are to a national audience by a sitting president of the United States. I include a chapter on historical speeches to illustrate historical analysis using the model. An attribute associated within the model implicitly, as discussed in Chapter 3, is the culture in which an audience has lived and its impact on prior experiences and cognition and perception. A challenge with historical study of persuasive speeches is to understand the historical context of the speech. The persuasive dynamics of such a speech cannot be removed from its culture when studying these dynamics. Much as the contemporary reader of this book is likely to understand concerns related to the fracking debate presented earlier, one needs to understand the historical context and culture present at the time of the speech. So, analysis necessarily includes such consideration.

Further, historical analysis should consider technologies available at a given period of time and the audience's familiarity with that technology. This attribute will necessarily affect analysis with the model since the model includes consideration of the medium used to disseminate the message. The audience's experience with a given technology affects how it uses that technology (Norman, 1988). I mentioned in Chapter 2, Pinker's (1997) observation that people develop mental images to help them process information. A mental image of an object or person may help one to visualize the object or person when it or the person is not present at a given moment. For example, one may discuss the difference between Granny Smith apples and Red Delicious apples without either being present, and if another has seen both and retains the image of both in their mind, they can visualize each and "see" their differences during the discussion. So, while a message may be delivered monomodally (using a medium that facilitates one mode of representation), an audience of such a message may integrate a mental image to compliment that mode, making it a multimodal experience for the audience.

Prior to the advent of television, radio was the dominant medium. Radio facilitates only audio; however, one may have an image in their mind of what the speaker looks like and exercises that image during the broadcast. This may be associated with the Visual Dominance attribute of the model; the brain attempts to develop an image when one is not present, and it can do so based on previous experiences with that object or person or situation. An historian or political scientist, for example, may find analysis over a period of time relative just to technologies available for dissemination of political speeches of interest and value. I call attention to this topic in this chapter. The first speech I analyze was broadcasted via radio, before television was invented; yet, the audience could have visualized the speaker, creating a multimodal message for it.

Any presidential speech or Congressional testimony tends to integrate a few elements of persuasion, even if it seems mostly to be informational. The speaker attempts to use the speech to unite the country as one relative to the policy or action of which the person is speaking while trying also to appear genuinely concerned about the nation's interests. Positioned as a leader, the speaker attempts to persuade the listeners to follow his policy and decisions. The tone of the speaker's voice, then, tends to be authoritative yet concerned.

As those who have seen my previous books know, I am interested in World War II. It was a period in which nations around the world engaged in war on a scale never seen before nor since as democracy fought off imperialism. Even before U.S. involvement in WWII, the nation was manufacturing materials to support the Allies in their efforts to turn back German and Japanese Imperialism. With his "Great Arsenal of Democracy speech," President Franklin Delano Roosevelt (F.D.R.) announced that he had authorized construction of several arsenals around the country that would develop munitions and act as warehouses for ammunition for the allies in the war. He framed this project around the fact that the world was facing a challenge to democracy from imperialist nations such as Germany and Japan. Generally, the speech encourages industry to change toward a war economy and lifting many restrictions on production and hiring of workers. The persuasive message, then, is to encourage industry and public to galvanize efforts toward helping fight against imperialism overseas.

Another important political speech is that of John F. Kennedy during the Cuban Missile Crisis. In it, he acknowledges to the U.S. public and the world that the Soviet Union has placed nuclear missiles in Cuba, less than 100 miles from U.S. mainland. The message is addressed to multiple national audiences—to the U.S. public to let them know of the situation and convince them that his policy is right, and to the Cuban public to persuade them to sympathize with U.S. policy and perceive it to be correct.

The third address is that of Ronald Reagan to the people of Germany near the end of Soviet occupation of East Germany. Tensions of the Cold War had eased considerably by the time he spoke in Berlin to encourage the Soviet Union to remove physical barriers to reform and material artifacts of discord. The message there is to "tear down this wall," encouraging democracy and other political reforms away from communism.

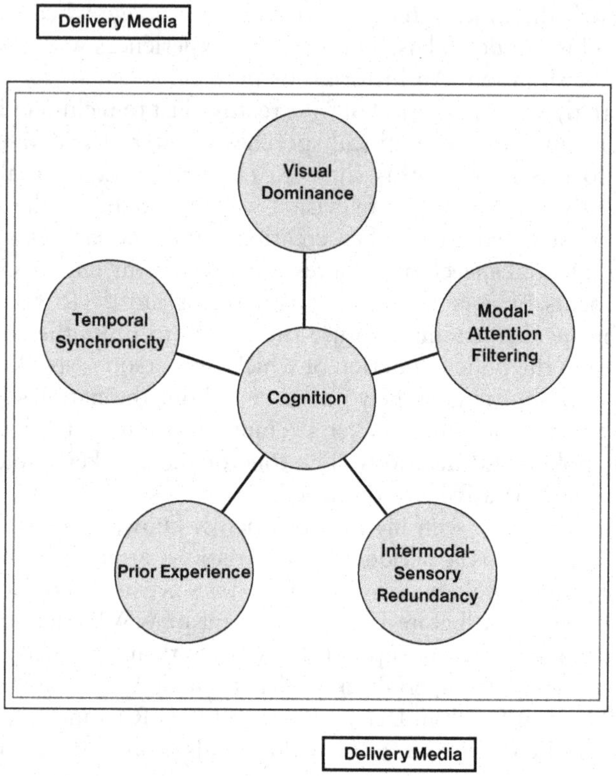

Delivery Media

Delivery Media

Figure 8.1 Model.

As I discuss each relative to the model I call attention to particular statements that are relevant to the analysis. A transcript of each speech is available in the Appendix; however, that is a print-linguistic representation of the speech, excluding multimodal attributes. All of the speeches are available via YouTube or the National Archives' website for viewing or listening. So, I draw on some of the attributes of the actual video or audio in the analyses.

Again, I provide the visual representation of the model as a reference point below.

The Great Arsenal of Democracy—December 29, 1940

Medium

The speech was actually among F.D.R.'s "Fireside Chat's," periodic speeches he would give to the nation via radio broadcast to keep citizens informed of policy and political developments between 1933 and 1944.

Television did not yet exist, but radio was a popular broadcast mechanism; many radio stations and networks had regular series and radio shows. The radio was generally placed in a common room, perhaps a living room that also had a fireplace. So, listeners might be sitting next to the radio while a warm fire blazed in the fireplace. The fireside chats were not a regular series; only 30 occurred during the 11-year period (an average of less than three per year), but they were among the first means by which a U.S. president spoke to a mass audience of citizens.

Modal Attention Filtering

Audio without any visual enhancement can help to focus attention; but it eliminates the visual dominance attribute of the model, except that a listener could visualize the president as he spoke because of images of him they had seen in print. Again, when an image is absent the mind attempts to create an image to help it process information. Nevertheless, the radio broadcast could filter other visual information that could be a distraction to the message, unless the listener was distracted by something at his or her home.

Prior Experience

I discuss the Prior Experience attribute of the model here with respect to both the medium and with respect to the message. As I indicated in Chapter 4, regarding the medium and technology, one's experience with a medium affects their ability to use it as a tool. This applies to both using it to create the message as well as using it as an audience of the message. Many people these days (21st century), for example, have difficulty listening to a radio broadcast of a sports event; they prefer to see video of the game, because they cannot visualize the action. The prevalence of television and video streaming online makes almost any sports event accessible through video; however, in 1940, everyone would have been more familiar with using radio to listen to a game and try to visualize the action in their mind. Because radio was the most common broadcast tool, the general public was very familiar with listening to it as a news source. Because there is just the one mode, intermodal sensory redundancy is limited, like visual dominance, to imagined visualization of the president speaking.

With respect to the message, the general public was familiar with the war going on in Europe and that Japan was an ally of Germany. There were several news stories about Germany's expansion into various territories and nations in Europe. The general public knew, also, of Adolph Hitler through print and radio broadcast news. The primary message that would be new to listeners was the scale to which the U.S. was in danger and the scale on which the U.S. would be assisting England and its allies in the war. F.D.R., in fact, acknowledges this danger very early in the message:

> Never before since Jamestown and Plymouth Rock has our American civilization been in such danger as now. For on September 27th, 1940—this year—by an agreement signed in Berlin, three powerful nations, two in Europe and one in Asia, joined themselves together in the threat that if the United States of America interfered with or blocked the expansion program of these three nations—a program aimed at world control—they would unite in ultimate action against the United States.
>
> The Nazi masters of Germany have made it clear that they intend not only to dominate all life and thought in their own country, but also to enslave the whole of Europe, and then to use the resources of Europe to dominate the rest of the world. It was only three weeks ago that their leader stated this: "There are two worlds that stand opposed to each other." And then in defiant reply to his opponents he said this: "Others are correct when they say: 'With this world we cannot ever reconcile ourselves.'" I can beat any other power in the world." So said the leader of the Nazis.

For the most part, citizens of the U.S. observed with interest the happenings in Europe, knowing that the Nazis were making considerable gains. However, the U.S. was "safe" from invasion because of the oceans. The U.S. also had touted its neutrality in the war and a general policy of isolationism. However, with the realization that the Nazis would try to dominate the World, and given their vast expansion to that point, more action was needed to defend the security of the U.S. He conveys this need as well:

> If Great Britain goes down, the Axis powers will control the Continents of Europe, Asia, Africa, Austral-Asia, and the high seas. And they will be in a position to bring enormous military and naval resources against this hemisphere. It is no exaggeration to say that all of us in all the Americas would be living at the point of a gun—a gun loaded with explosive bullets, economic as well as military. We should enter upon a new and terrible era in which the whole world, our hemisphere included, would be run by threats of brute force. And to survive in such a world, we would have to convert ourselves permanently into a militaristic power on the basis of war economy.

Finally, he acknowledges the scale on which the assistance to Great Britain will occur and attempts to persuade the citizens that it is the right policy as well as persuade them to participate fully.

> We are planning our own defense with the utmost urgency, and in its vast scale we must integrate the war needs of Britain and the other

free nations which are resisting aggression. This is not a matter of sentiment or of controversial personal opinion. It is a matter of realistic, practical military policy, based on the advice of our military experts who are in close touch with existing warfare. These military and naval experts and the members of the Congress and the Administration have a single-minded purpose: the defense of the United States.

This nation is making a great effort to produce everything that is necessary in this emergency, and with all possible speed. And this great effort requires great sacrifice. I would ask no one to defend a democracy which in turn would not defend every one in the nation against want and privation. The strength of this nation shall not be diluted by the failure of the government to protect the economic well-being of its citizens. If our capacity to produce is limited by machines, it must ever be remembered that these machines are operated by the skill and the stamina of the workers.

As the government is determined to protect the rights of the workers, so the nation has a right to expect that the men who man the machines will discharge their full responsibilities to the urgent needs of defense. The worker possesses the same human dignity and is entitled to the same security of position as the engineer or the manager or the owner. For the workers provide the human power that turns out the destroyers, and the planes, and the tanks. The nation expects our defense industries to continue operation without interruption by strikes or lockouts. It expects and insists that management and workers will reconcile their differences by voluntary or legal means, to continue to produce the supplies that are so sorely needed. And on the economic side of our great defense program, we are, as you know, bending every effort to maintain stability of prices and with that the stability of the cost of living.

Conclusion

The speech appeals to mirror neurons, because the president is an expert on national policy and security. The U.S. audience values his position and wants to support it, especially given the threat to national security even though the U.S. is not yet in the War. It becomes apparent to the audience that if Great Britain and its allies cannot win the War, freedoms that they have enjoyed are endangered. Consequently, the reward neural appeal is that freedom and democracy will win if all in the audience unite to assist in the allied war effort against Nazi Germany and Imperialist Japan.

Cuban Missile Crisis—October 22, 1960

An interesting attribute of this message by John F. Kennedy is that he addresses both U.S. citizens and Cuban citizens. The message is broadcasted to both audiences.

Medium

This speech was delivered via television as well as radio. Television was still emerging as a communication tool, and it integrated both audio and visual attributes. As we see sometimes even today, the president sat at his official table in the Oval Office, wearing a suit. So, the image of the president was very official.

Modal Attention Filtering

While the medium facilitates both audio and visual, the emphasis on the audio is clear, because the president does not stand or move about the room as he speaks. He sits at the desk throughout the entire speech; consequently, there is little visual distraction. Like the radio broadcast, the viewer focuses on the audio; however, the viewer does not have to imagine the speaker; he or she can clearly see the speaker. However, the viewer also sees only the president's face and upper body generally as he reads the message; this filters the video portion of the message. The viewer can focus on a limited amount of visual information while listening to the words of his speech.

Prior Experience

The world knew of the rise of nuclear capabilities, and many people had begun training for nuclear war. Bomb shelters existed and civil defense personnel routinely held drills to encourage practicing for such a war. The general public; however, was unaware of the potential danger the U.S. faced from the Soviet Union. Again, there was a large ocean between the U.S. and any other nation that could be aggressive against the U.S.

People, also, knew of the failed attempts to unite Cuba with democracy. However, it was a small island and few feared it on its own. However, as the Soviet Union began placing strategic missiles in Cuba, the risk of a nuclear threat grew exponentially. Missiles would be less than 100 miles from U.S. mainland and capable of reaching well into the country. So, the message that would be new to the public would be of that proximity of threat. Kennedy makes that statement very early in the message:

> Within the past week, unmistakable evidence has established the fact that a series of offensive missile sites is now in preparation on that imprisoned island. The purpose of these bases can be none other than to provide a nuclear strike capability against the Western Hemisphere.
>
> Upon receiving the first preliminary hard information of this nature last Tuesday morning at 9 A.M., I directed that our surveillance be stepped up. And having now confirmed and completed our evaluation of the evidence and our decision on a course of action, this Government feels obliged to report this new crisis to you in fullest detail.

Kennedy goes on to make a case that the Soviet Union has lied and is taking an offensive positioning with these missiles:

> This action also contradicts the repeated assurances of Soviet spokesmen, both publicly and privately delivered, that the arms buildup in Cuba would retain its original defensive character, and that the Soviet Union had no need or desire to station strategic missiles. on the territory of any other nation.
>
> The size of this undertaking makes clear that it has been planned for some months. Yet, only last month, after I had made clear the distinction between any introduction of ground-to-ground missiles and the existence of defensive antiaircraft missiles, the Soviet Government publicly stated on September 11 that, and I quote, "the armaments and military equipment sent to Cuba are designed exclusively for defensive purposes," that there is, and I quote the Soviet Government, "there is no need for the Soviet Government to shift its weapons for a retaliatory blow to any other country, for instance Cuba," and that, and I quote their government, "the Soviet Union has so powerful rockets to carry these nuclear warheads that there is no need to search for sites for them beyond the boundaries of the Soviet Union."

That statement was false.

There is persuasive rhetoric in this statement, because he must convince the public that the Soviet Union is the aggressor and has lied, thereby positioning the U.S. and its new policy in the right. That understanding will help unite the citizens.

Kennedy also alludes to lessons learned from the preface of World War II and how the U.S. has tried to exercise restraint.

> The 1930's taught us a clear lesson: aggressive conduct, if allowed to go unchecked and unchallenged, ultimately leads to war. This nation is opposed to war. We are also true to our word. Our unswerving objective, therefore, must be to prevent the use of these missiles against this or any other country, and to secure their withdrawal or elimination from the Western Hemisphere.
>
> Our policy has been one of patience and restraint, as befits a peaceful and powerful nation which leads a worldwide alliance.

As indicated above, he also speaks directly to the people of Cuba in an effort to galvanize them with regard to the U.S.' righteousness.

> Finally, I want to say a few words to the captive people of Cuba, to whom this speech is being directly carried by special radio facilities. I speak to you as a friend, as one who knows of your deep attachment to your fatherland, as one who shares your aspirations for liberty

and justice for all. And I have watched and the American people have watched with deep sorrow how your nationalist revolution was betrayed—and how your fatherland fell under foreign domination. Now your leaders are no longer Cuban leaders inspired by Cuban ideals. They are puppets and agents of an international conspiracy which has turned Cuba against your friends and neighbors in the Americas, and turned it into the first Latin American country to become a target for nuclear war—the first Latin American country to have these weapons on its soil.

These new weapons are not in your interest. They contribute nothing to your peace and well-being. They can only undermine it. But this country has no wish to cause you to suffer or to impose any system upon you. We know that your lives and land are being used as pawns by those who deny your freedom. Many times in the past, the Cuban people have risen to throw out tyrants who destroyed their liberty. And I have no doubt that most Cubans today look forward to the time when they will be truly free—free from foreign domination, free to choose their own leaders, free to select their own system, free to own their own land, free to speak and write and worship without fear or degradation. And then shall Cuba be welcomed back to the society of free nations and to the associations of this hemisphere.

He ends with the reassurance of U.S.' righteousness:

Our goal is not the victory of might, but the vindication of right; not peace at the expense of freedom, but both peace and freedom, here in this hemisphere, and, we hope, around the world. God willing, that goal will be achieved.

Given the audiences' memories, stored in their hippocampus, of what happened in the years before World War II and a similar occurrence appearing to happen in this situation, as presented by Kennedy, the audience would perceive a threat from the Soviet Union. This would provoke fear, related to the amygdala and the need for action to address the threat.

Intermodal Sensory Redundancy and Temporal Synchronicity

Intermodal redundancy and Temporal synchronicity may be considered together since television facilitates visual and audio. The audience can see Kennedy's expression of authoritativeness and frustration with the Soviet Union as he reads his prepared speech. The two—facial expression and words-occur together.

Conclusion

This speech, addressed to both U.S. and Cuban citizens, appeals to mirror neurons in much the same way that F.D.R.'s speech did. The audience values the president's position and wants to support the policy because it pertains to national security and a real threat to it. The audience has the same values as the president represents in the message. The reward (reward neurons), of course, to both audiences is the continued security of freedoms of democracy and life. Given the nuclear nature of the threat and an understanding of the effect of nuclear bombs based on the bombing of two Japanese cities to end World War II, each member of the audience is concerned about his or her life, not just national security. So, there is something in the message that appeals to every person in the audience on a personal level—their own life.

The Wall—1987

In the late-1980s, military and political tensions between the Soviet Union and the U.S. were settling down largely because of a series of nuclear arms treaties that limited the number of weapons a nation could have while also reducing the number that existed. A division still existed, but negotiations toward furthering peaceful relations were occurring. President Reagan was one of several presidents to visit Berlin, Germany during his presidency. Berlin not only represented considerable history generally, but it was the material location where east (Communism) and west (Democracy) were divided by a wall built in 1961 to discourage people from running from the eastern side of the city to the western side, across a line established to demarcate the Soviet-controlled sector of the city and the U.S.-controlled sector after World War II.

Reagan's speech reviews much of the history of the Cold War, but he announces to the world (not just an American audience) further invitation to the Soviet Union to establish peace and freedoms. He explicitly makes this invitation near the end of the speech:

> And I invite Mr. Gorbachev: Let us work to bring the Eastern and Western parts of the city closer together, so that all the inhabitants of all Berlin can enjoy the benefits that come with life in one of the great cities of the world.
>
> To open Berlin still further to all Europe, East and West, let us expand the vital air access to this city, finding ways of making commercial air service to Berlin more convenient, more comfortable, and more economical. We look to the day when West Berlin can become one of the chief aviation hubs in all central Europe.
>
> With—With our French—With our French and British partners, the United States is prepared to help bring international meetings to

Berlin. It would be only fitting for Berlin to serve as the site of United Nations meetings, or world conferences on human rights and arms control, or other issues that call for international cooperation.

I analyze the speech relative to the model. However, the reader should note a pattern emerging with the selection of speeches and their analyses in this chapter—I started with a speech that not only was limited to radio broadcast but was addressed to the U.S. audience, and I have moved to speeches that were broadcast via television and to audiences that included U.S. as well as audiences of other nations. With each move, the message requires additional multimodal persuasive rhetoric to affect an influence.

Medium

This speech was delivered via television and radio to many nations around the world. President Reagan even acknowledges this early in the speech to let the audiences know of the reach of this message, and perhaps, to let the audiences know that he will speak to each nation.

Our gathering today is being broadcast throughout Western Europe and North America. I understand that it is being seen and heard as well in the East. To those listening throughout Eastern Europe, I extend my warmest greetings and the good will of the American people. To those listening in East Berlin, a special word: Although I cannot be with you, I address my remarks to you just as surely as to those standing here before me. For I join you, as I join your fellow countrymen in the West, in this firm, this unalterable belief: Es gibt nur ein Berlin. [There is only one Berlin.]

Consequently, there can be a visual dominance element as well as audio, as was the case with Kennedy's speech. However, the audience sees more than just the President's upper body and face. The President is positioned in front of the Berlin Wall, and some of those in attendance can be seen as well.

Modal Attention Filtering

There is less filtering of visual elements in this speech than in Kennedy's speech. This is to contribute to the intermodal redundancy and temporal synchronicity attributes. The people present on site, experience the chill in the air, but the millions, perhaps billions, of others watching do not. So, this raises another interesting attribute of the various audiences. Some experience more modes than others do.

Prior Experience

As mentioned above, the audience is aware of the Cold War tensions that have been going on for the 35-odd years prior to this speech. Tensions were still on the rise at the time of Kennedy's speech, but they have quieted a bit as of Reagan's speech because of public concern and political posturing to avoid looking like an aggressor. Many in the audience will have recalled the actual building of the wall and people being shot as they tried to cross the wall in its early years.

The Cold War created much fear in people all over the world such that most any escalation of tension caused genuine concern about life in general. The Cuban Missile Crisis, in fact, had occurred less than 25 years earlier. So, the amygdala for anyone over the age of 35 would be on alert for much of this period, and the hippocampus would have several fearful memories on which to draw.

Intermodal Redundancy and Temporal Synchronicity

The audience sees the President speaking as a wall exists behind him. Indeed, he refers to the wall a few times in the speech, using it very much as a visual aide. It represents much of the history of the Cold War. Between the audio of his speech and the visual images of the President and the wall the audience process several messages—historical and present—about war and peace.

The President is dressed warmly as are most that can be seen; so, the audience that is on site experiences the same cold as the President does. Many of those not present and watching from their warm home likely understand what a chill in the air feels like and can empathize (mirror neurons). So, there is a connection with the audience on site.

Conclusion

I have already mentioned a few elements associated with mirror neurons. Another that I have not yet mentioned is the President's use of the German language within the speech. Much as Kennedy did during his own speech in Berlin ("I am a Berliner"), Reagan seeks to appeal to the German audience's mirror neurons by aligning himself with that audience via language. Indeed, language is a primary tool for assimilating with an audience; one who speaks the same language as an audience makes the audience feel more at home—safe.

The appeal to Reward Neurons is that of world peace and further reduction of tensions.

Appendix

The Great Arsenal of Democracy Speech:
December 29, 1940

Franklin Delano Roosevelt

Retrieved from http://www.americanrhetoric.com/speeches/fdrarsenalof
democracy.html. American Rhetoric: Top 100 Speeches.
  March 14, 2008

My friends:

This is not a fireside chat on war. It is a talk on national security; because the nub of the whole purpose of your President is to keep you now,
and your children later, and your grandchildren much later, out of a last-
ditch war for the preservation of American independence, and all of the
things that American independence means to you and to me and to ours.

Tonight, in the presence of a world crisis, my mind goes back eight years
to a night in the midst of a domestic crisis. It was a time when the wheels of
American industry were grinding to a full stop, when the whole banking
system of our country had ceased to function. I well remember that while
I sat in my study in the White House, preparing to talk with the people of
the United States, I had before my eyes the picture of all those Americans
with whom I was talking. I saw the workmen in the mills, the mines, the
factories, the girl behind the counter, the small shopkeeper, the farmer
doing his spring plowing, the widows and the old men wondering about
their life's savings. I tried to convey to the great mass of American people
what the banking crisis meant to them in their daily lives.

Tonight, I want to do the same thing, with the same people, in this
new crisis which faces America. We met the issue of 1933 with courage and realism. We face this new crisis, this new threat to the security
of our nation, with the same courage and realism. Never before since
Jamestown and Plymouth Rock has our American civilization been in
such danger as now. For on September 27th, 1940—this year—by an
agreement signed in Berlin, three powerful nations, two in Europe and
one in Asia, joined themselves together in the threat that if the United
States of America interfered with or blocked the expansion program of
these three nations—a program aimed at world control—they would
unite in ultimate action against the United States.

The Nazi masters of Germany have made it clear that they intend not
only to dominate all life and thought in their own country, but also to
enslave the whole of Europe, and then to use the resources of Europe to
dominate the rest of the world. It was only three weeks ago that their
leader stated this: "There are two worlds that stand opposed to each

other." And then in defiant reply to his opponents he said this: "Others are correct when they say: 'With this world we cannot ever reconcile ourselves.' I can beat any other power in the world." So said the leader of the Nazis.

In other words, the Axis not merely admits but the Axis proclaims that there can be no ultimate peace between their philosophy—their philosophy of government—and our philosophy of government. In view of the nature of this undeniable threat, it can be asserted, properly and categorically, that the United States has no right or reason to encourage talk of peace until the day shall come when there is a clear intention on the part of the aggressor nations to abandon all thought of dominating or conquering the world.

At this moment the forces of the States that are leagued against all peoples who live in freedom are being held away from our shores. The Germans and the Italians are being blocked on the other side of the Atlantic by the British and by the Greeks, and by thousands of soldiers and sailors who were able to escape from subjugated countries. In Asia the Japanese are being engaged by the Chinese nation in another great defense. In the Pacific Ocean is our fleet.

Some of our people like to believe that wars in Europe and in Asia are of no concern to us. But it is a matter of most vital concern to us that European and Asiatic war-makers should not gain control of the oceans which lead to this hemisphere. One hundred and seventeen years ago the Monroe Doctrine was conceived by our government as a measure of defense in the face of a threat against this hemisphere by an alliance in Continental Europe. Thereafter, we stood guard in the Atlantic, with the British as neighbors. There was no treaty. There was no "unwritten agreement." And yet there was the feeling, proven correct by history, that we as neighbors could settle any disputes in peaceful fashion. And the fact is that during the whole of this time the Western Hemisphere has remained free from aggression from Europe or from Asia.

Does anyone seriously believe that we need to fear attack anywhere in the Americas while a free Britain remains our most powerful naval neighbor in the Atlantic? And does anyone seriously believe, on the other hand, that we could rest easy if the Axis powers were our neighbors there? If Great Britain goes down, the Axis powers will control the Continents of Europe, Asia, Africa, Austral-Asia, and the high seas. And they will be in a position to bring enormous military and naval resources against this hemisphere. It is no exaggeration to say that all of us in all the Americas would be living at the point of a gun—a gun loaded with explosive bullets, economic as well as military. We should enter upon a new and terrible era in which the whole world, our hemisphere included, would be run by threats of brute force. And to survive in such a world, we would have to convert ourselves permanently into a militaristic power on the basis of war economy.

Some of us like to believe that even if Britain falls, we are still safe, because of the broad expanse of the Atlantic and of the Pacific. But the width of those oceans is not what it was in the days of clipper ships. At one point between Africa and Brazil the distance is less than it is from Washington to Denver, Colorado, five hours for the latest type of bomber. And at the north end of the Pacific Ocean, America and Asia almost touch each other. Why, even today we have planes that could fly from the British Isles to New England and back again without refueling. And remember that the range of the modern bomber is ever being increased.

During the past week many people in all parts of the nation have told me what they wanted me to say tonight. Almost all of them expressed a courageous desire to hear the plain truth about the gravity of the situation. One telegram, however, expressed the attitude of the small minority who want to see no evil and hear no evil, even though they know in their hearts that evil exists. That telegram begged me not to tell again of the ease with which our American cities could be bombed by any hostile power which had gained bases in this Western Hemisphere. The gist of that telegram was: "Please, Mr. President, don't frighten us by telling us the facts." Frankly and definitely there is danger ahead—danger against which we must prepare. But we well know that we cannot escape danger, or the fear of danger, by crawling into bed and pulling the covers over our heads.

Some nations of Europe were bound by solemn nonintervention pacts with Germany. Other nations were assured by Germany that they need never fear invasion. Nonintervention pact or not, the fact remains that they were attacked, overrun, thrown into modern slavery at an hour's notice—or even without any notice at all. As an exiled leader of one of these nations said to me the other day, "The notice was a minus quantity. It was given to my government two hours after German troops had poured into my country in a hundred places." The fate of these nations tells us what it means to live at the point of a Nazi gun.

The Nazis have justified such actions by various pious frauds. One of these frauds is the claim that they are occupying a nation for the purpose of "restoring order." Another is that they are occupying or controlling a nation on the excuse that they are "protecting it" against the aggression of somebody else. For example, Germany has said that she was occupying Belgium to save the Belgians from the British. Would she then hesitate to say to any South American country: "We are occupying you to protect you from aggression by the United States"? Belgium today is being used as an invasion base against Britain, now fighting for its life. And any South American country, in Nazi hands, would always constitute a jumping off place for German attack on any one of the other republics of this hemisphere.

Analyze for yourselves the future of two other places even nearer to Germany if the Nazis won. Could Ireland hold out? Would Irish freedom be permitted as an amazing pet exception in an unfree world? Or the islands of the Azores, which still fly the flag of Portugal after five centuries? You and I think of Hawaii as an outpost of defense in the Pacific. And yet the Azores are closer to our shores in the Atlantic than Hawaii is on the other side.

There are those who say that the Axis powers would never have any desire to attack the Western Hemisphere. That is the same dangerous form of wishful thinking which has destroyed the powers of resistance of so many conquered peoples. The plain facts are that the Nazis have proclaimed, time and again, that all other races are their inferiors and therefore subject to their orders. And most important of all, the vast resources and wealth of this American hemisphere constitute the most tempting loot in all of the round world.

Let us no longer blind ourselves to the undeniable fact that the evil forces which have crushed and undermined and corrupted so many others are already within our own gates. Your government knows much about them and every day is ferreting them out. Their secret emissaries are active in our own and in neighboring countries. They seek to stir up suspicion and dissension, to cause internal strife. They try to turn capital against labor, and vice versa. They try to reawaken long slumbering racial and religious enmities which should have no place in this country. They are active in every group that promotes intolerance. They exploit for their own ends our own natural abhorrence of war. These trouble-breeders have but one purpose. It is to divide our people, to divide them into hostile groups and to destroy our unity and shatter our will to defend ourselves.

There are also American citizens, many of them in high places, who, unwittingly in most cases, are aiding and abetting the work of these agents. I do not charge these American citizens with being foreign agents. But I do charge them with doing exactly the kind of work that the dictators want done in the United States. These people not only believe that we can save our own skins by shutting our eyes to the fate of other nations. Some of them go much further than that. They say that we can and should become the friends and even the partners of the Axis powers. Some of them even suggest that we should imitate the methods of the dictatorships. But Americans never can and never will do that.

The experience of the past two years has proven beyond doubt that no nation can appease the Nazis. No man can tame a tiger into a kitten by stroking it. There can be no appeasement with ruthlessness. There can be no reasoning with an incendiary bomb. We know now that a nation can have peace with the Nazis only at the price of total surrender. Even the people of Italy have been forced to become accomplices of the Nazis; but at this moment they do not know how soon they will be embraced to death by their allies.

The American appeasers ignore the warning to be found in the fate of Austria, Czechoslovakia, Poland, Norway, Belgium, the Netherlands, Denmark, and France. They tell you that the Axis powers are going to win anyway; that all of this bloodshed in the world could be saved, that the United States might just as well throw its influence into the scale of a dictated peace and get the best out of it that we can. They call it a "negotiated peace." Nonsense! Is it a negotiated peace if a gang of outlaws surrounds your community and on threat of extermination makes you pay tribute to save your own skins? For such a dictated peace would be no peace at all. It would be only another armistice, leading to the most gigantic armament race and the most devastating trade wars in all history. And in these contests the Americas would offer the only real resistance to the Axis power. With all their vaunted efficiency, with all their parade of pious purpose in this war, there are still in their background the concentration camp and the servants of God in chains.

The history of recent years proves that the shootings and the chains and the concentration camps are not simply the transient tools but the very altars of modern dictatorships. They may talk of a "new order" in the world, but what they have in mind is only a revival of the oldest and the worst tyranny. In that there is no liberty, no religion, no hope. The proposed "new order" is the very opposite of a United States of Europe or a United States of Asia. It is not a government based upon the consent of the governed. It is not a union of ordinary, self-respecting men and women to protect themselves and their freedom and their dignity from oppression. It is an unholy alliance of power and pelf to dominate and to enslave the human race.

The British people and their allies today are conducting an active war against this unholy alliance. Our own future security is greatly dependent on the outcome of that fight. Our ability to "keep out of war" is going to be affected by that outcome. Thinking in terms of today and tomorrow, I make the direct statement to the American people that there is far less chance of the United States getting into war if we do all we can now to support the nations defending themselves against attack by the Axis than if we acquiesce in their defeat, submit tamely to an Axis victory, and wait our turn to be the object of attack in another war later on.

If we are to be completely honest with ourselves, we must admit that there is risk in any course we may take. But I deeply believe that the great majority of our people agree that the course that I advocate involves the least risk now and the greatest hope for world peace in the future.

The people of Europe who are defending themselves do not ask us to do their fighting. They ask us for the implements of war, the planes, the tanks, the guns, the freighters which will enable them to fight for their liberty and for our security. Emphatically, we must get these weapons to them, get them to them in sufficient volume and quickly enough so that we and our children will be saved the agony and suffering of war which others have had to endure.

Let not the defeatists tell us that it is too late. It will never be earlier. Tomorrow will be later than today.

Certain facts are self-evident.

In a military sense Great Britain and the British Empire are today the spearhead of resistance to world conquest. And they are putting up a fight which will live forever in the story of human gallantry. There is no demand for sending an American expeditionary force outside our own borders. There is no intention by any member of your government to send such a force. You can therefore, nail, nail any talk about sending armies to Europe as deliberate untruth. Our national policy is not directed toward war. Its sole purpose is to keep war away from our country and away from our people.

Democracy's fight against world conquest is being greatly aided, and must be more greatly aided, by the rearmament of the United States and by sending every ounce and every ton of munitions and supplies that we can possibly spare to help the defenders who are in the front lines. And it is no more un-neutral for us to do that than it is for Sweden, Russia, and other nations near Germany to send steel and ore and oil and other war materials into Germany every day in the week.

We are planning our own defense with the utmost urgency, and in its vast scale we must integrate the war needs of Britain and the other free nations which are resisting aggression. This is not a matter of sentiment or of controversial personal opinion. It is a matter of realistic, practical military policy, based on the advice of our military experts who are in close touch with existing warfare. These military and naval experts and the members of the Congress and the Administration have a single-minded purpose: the defense of the United States.

This nation is making a great effort to produce everything that is necessary in this emergency, and with all possible speed. And this great effort requires great sacrifice. I would ask no one to defend a democracy which in turn would not defend every one in the nation against want and privation. The strength of this nation shall not be diluted by the failure of the government to protect the economic well-being of its citizens. If our capacity to produce is limited by machines, it must ever be remembered that these machines are operated by the skill and the stamina of the workers.

As the government is determined to protect the rights of the workers, so the nation has a right to expect that the men who man the machines will discharge their full responsibilities to the urgent needs of defense. The worker possesses the same human dignity and is entitled to the same security of position as the engineer or the manager or the owner. For the workers provide the human power that turns out the destroyers, and the planes, and the tanks. The nation expects our defense industries to continue operation without interruption by strikes or lockouts. It expects and insists that management and workers will reconcile their differences by voluntary or legal means, to continue to produce the supplies that are so sorely needed. And on the economic side of our great defense program, we are, as you know, bending every effort to maintain stability of prices and with that the stability of the cost of living.

Nine days ago I announced the setting up of a more effective organization to direct our gigantic efforts to increase the production of munitions. The appropriation of vast sums of money and a well-coordinated executive direction of our defense efforts are not in themselves enough. Guns, planes, ships, and many other things have to be built in the factories and the arsenals of America. They have to be produced by workers and managers and engineers with the aid of machines which in turn have to be built by hundreds of thousands of workers throughout the land. In this great work there has been splendid cooperation between the government and industry and labor. And I am very thankful.

American industrial genius, unmatched throughout all the world in the solution of production problems, has been called upon to bring its resources and its talents into action. Manufacturers of watches, of farm implements, of Linotypes and cash registers and automobiles, and sewing machines and lawn mowers and locomotives, are now making fuses and bomb packing crates and telescope mounts and shells and pistols and tanks.

But all of our present efforts are not enough. We must have more ships, more guns, more planes—more of everything. And this can be accomplished only if we discard the notion of "business as usual." This job cannot be done merely by superimposing on the existing productive facilities the added requirements of the nation for defense. Our defense efforts must not be blocked by those who fear the future consequences of surplus plant capacity. The possible consequences of failure of our defense efforts now are much more to be feared. And after the present needs of our defense are past, a proper handling of the country's peacetime needs will require all of the new productive capacity, if not still more. No pessimistic policy about the future of America shall delay the immediate expansion of those industries essential to defense. We need them.

I want to make it clear that it is the purpose of the nation to build now with all possible speed every machine, every arsenal, every factory that we need to manufacture our defense material. We have the men, the skill, the wealth, and above all, the will. I am confident that if and when production of consumer or luxury goods in certain industries requires the use of machines and raw materials that are essential for defense purposes, then such production must yield, and will gladly yield, to our primary and compelling purpose.

So I appeal to the owners of plants, to the managers, to the workers, to our own government employees to put every ounce of effort into producing these munitions swiftly and without stint. With this appeal I give you the pledge that all of us who are officers of your government will devote ourselves to the same whole-hearted extent to the great task that lies ahead.

As planes and ships and guns and shells are produced, your government, with its defense experts, can then determine how best to use them to defend this hemisphere. The decision as to how much shall be sent abroad and how much shall remain at home must be made on the basis of our overall military necessities.

We must be the great arsenal of democracy.

For us this is an emergency as serious as war itself. We must apply ourselves to our task with the same resolution, the same sense of urgency, the same spirit of patriotism and sacrifice as we would show were we at war.

We have furnished the British great material support and we will furnish far more in the future. There will be no "bottlenecks" in our determination to aid Great Britain. No dictator, no combination of dictators, will weaken that determination by threats of how they will construe that determination. The British have received invaluable military support from the heroic Greek Army and from the forces of all the governments in exile. Their strength is growing. It is the strength of men and women who value their freedom more highly than they value their lives.

I believe that the Axis powers are not going to win this war. I base that belief on the latest and best of information.

We have no excuse for defeatism. We have every good reason for hope—hope for peace, yes, and hope for the defense of our civilization and for the building of a better civilization in the future. I have the profound conviction that the American people are now determined to put forth a mightier effort than they have ever yet made to increase our production of all the implements of defense, to meet the threat to our democratic faith.

As President of the United States, I call for that national effort. I call for it in the name of this nation which we love and honor and which we are privileged and proud to serve. I call upon our people with absolute confidence that our common cause will greatly succeed.

John F. Kennedy

Cuban Missile Crisis Address to the Nation
   delivered 22 October 1962
   Retrievedfromhttp://www.americanrhetoric.com/speeches/fdrarsenalof democracy.html. American Rhetoric: Top 100 Speeches

*[AUTHENTICITY CERTIFIED: Text version below
transcribed directly from audio.]*

Good evening, my fellow citizens:

This Government, as promised, has maintained the closest surveillance of the Soviet military buildup on the island of Cuba. Within the past week, unmistakable evidence has established the fact that a series of offensive missile sites is now in preparation on that imprisoned island. The purpose of these bases can be none other than to provide a nuclear strike capability against the Western Hemisphere.

Upon receiving the first preliminary hard information of this nature last Tuesday morning at 9 A.M., I directed that our surveillance be stepped up. And having now confirmed and completed our evaluation of the evidence and our decision on a course of action, this Government feels obliged to report this new crisis to you in fullest detail.

The characteristics of these new missile sites indicate two distinct types of installations. Several of them include medium range ballistic missiles, capable of carrying a nuclear warhead for a distance of more than 1,000 nautical miles. Each of these missiles, in short, is capable of striking Washington, D. C., the Panama Canal, Cape Canaveral, Mexico City, or any other city in the southeastern part of the United States, in Central America, or in the Caribbean area.

Additional sites not yet completed appear to be designed for intermediate range ballistic missiles—capable of traveling more than twice as far—and thus capable of striking most of the major cities in the Western Hemisphere, ranging as far north as Hudson Bay, Canada, and as far south as Lima, Peru. In addition, jet bombers, capable of carrying nuclear weapons, are now being uncrated and assembled in Cuba, while the necessary air bases are being prepared.

This urgent transformation of Cuba into an important strategic base— by the presence of these large, long-range, and clearly offensive weapons of sudden mass destruction—constitutes an explicit threat to the peace and security of all the Americas, in flagrant and deliberate defiance of the Rio Pact of 1947, the traditions of this nation and hemisphere, the joint resolution of the 87th Congress, the Charter of the United Nations, and my own public warnings to the Soviets on September 4 and 13. This action also contradicts the repeated assurances of Soviet spokesmen, both publicly and privately delivered, that the arms buildup in Cuba would retain its original defensive character, and that the Soviet Union had no need or desire to station strategic missiles. on the territory of any other nation.

The size of this undertaking makes clear that it has been planned for some months. Yet, only last month, after I had made clear the distinction between any introduction of ground-to-ground missiles and the existence of defensive antiaircraft missiles, the Soviet Government publicly stated on September 11 that, and I quote, "the armaments and military equipment sent to Cuba are designed exclusively for defensive purposes," that there is, and I quote the Soviet Government, "there is no need for the Soviet Government to shift its weapons for a retaliatory blow to any other country, for instance Cuba," and that, and I quote their government, "the Soviet Union has so powerful rockets to carry these nuclear warheads that there is no need to search for sites for them beyond the boundaries of the Soviet Union."

That statement was false.

Only last Thursday, as evidence of this rapid offensive buildup was already in my hand, Soviet Foreign Minister Gromyko told me in my office that he was instructed to make it clear once again, as he said his government had already done, that Soviet assistance to Cuba, and I quote, "pursued solely the purpose of contributing to the defense capabilities of Cuba," that, and I quote him, "training by Soviet specialists of Cuban nationals in handling defensive armaments was by no means offensive, and if it were otherwise," Mr. Gromyko went on, "the Soviet Government would never become involved in rendering such assistance."

That statement also was false.

Neither the United States of America nor the world community of nations can tolerate deliberate deception and offensive threats on the part of any nation, large or small. We no longer live in a world where only the actual firing of weapons represents a sufficient challenge to a nation's security to constitute maximum peril. Nuclear weapons are so destructive and ballistic missiles are so swift, that any substantially increased possibility of their use or any sudden change in their deployment may well be regarded as a definite threat to peace.

For many years, both the Soviet Union and the United States, recognizing this fact, have deployed strategic nuclear weapons with great care, never upsetting the precarious status quo which insured that these weapons would not be used in the absence of some vital challenge. Our own strategic missiles have never been transferred to the territory of any other nation under a cloak of secrecy and deception; and our history—unlike that of the Soviets since the end of World War II—demonstrates that we have no desire to dominate or conquer any other nation or impose our system upon its people. Nevertheless, American citizens have become adjusted to living daily on the bull's-eye of Soviet missiles located inside the U.S.S.R. or in submarines.

In that sense, missiles in Cuba add to an already clear and present danger—although it should be noted the nations of Latin America have never previously been subjected to a potential nuclear threat. But this secret, swift, extraordinary buildup of Communist missiles—in an area well known to have a special and historical relationship to the United States and the nations of the Western Hemisphere, in violation of Soviet assurances, and in defiance of American and hemispheric policy—this sudden, clandestine decision to station strategic weapons for the first time outside of Soviet soil—is a deliberately provocative and unjustified change in the status quo which cannot be accepted by this country, if our courage and our commitments are ever to be trusted again by either friend or foe.

The 1930's taught us a clear lesson: aggressive conduct, if allowed to go unchecked and unchallenged, ultimately leads to war. This nation is opposed to war. We are also true to our word. Our unswerving objective, therefore, must be to prevent the use of these missiles against this or any other country, and to secure their withdrawal or elimination from the Western Hemisphere.

Our policy has been one of patience and restraint, as befits a peaceful and powerful nation which leads a worldwide alliance. We have been determined not to be diverted from our central concerns by mere irritants and fanatics. But now further action is required, and it is under way; and these actions may only be the beginning. We will not prematurely or unnecessarily risk the costs of worldwide nuclear war in which even the fruits of victory would be ashes in our mouth; but neither will we shrink from that risk at any time it must be faced.

Acting, therefore, in the defense of our own security and of the entire Western Hemisphere, and under the authority entrusted to me by the Constitution as endorsed by the Resolution of the Congress, I have directed that the following initial steps be taken immediately:

First: To halt this offensive buildup a strict quarantine on all offensive military equipment under shipment to Cuba is being initiated. All ships of any kind bound for Cuba from whatever nation or port will, if found to contain cargoes of offensive weapons, be turned back. This quarantine will be extended, if needed, to other types of cargo and carriers. We are not at this time, however, denying the necessities of life as the Soviets attempted to do in their Berlin blockade of 1948.

Second: I have directed the continued and increased close surveillance of Cuba and its military buildup. The foreign ministers of the OAS [Organization of American States], in their communiqué' of October 6, rejected secrecy on such matters in this hemisphere. Should these offensive military preparations continue, thus increasing the threat to the hemisphere, further action will be justified. I have directed the Armed Forces to prepare for any eventualities; and I trust that in the interest of both the Cuban people and the Soviet technicians at the sites, the hazards to all concerned of continuing this threat will be recognized.

Third: It shall be the policy of this nation to regard any nuclear missile launched from Cuba against any nation in the Western Hemisphere as an attack by the Soviet Union on the United States, requiring a full retaliatory response upon the Soviet Union.

Fourth: As a necessary military precaution, I have reinforced our base at Guantanamo, evacuated today the dependents of our personnel there, and ordered additional military units to be on a standby alert basis.

Fifth: We are calling tonight for an immediate meeting of the Organ[ization] of Consultation under the Organization of American States, to consider this threat to hemispheric security and to invoke articles 6 and 8 of the Rio Treaty in support of all necessary action. The United Nations Charter allows for regional security arrangements, and the nations of this hemisphere decided long ago against the military presence of outside powers. Our other allies around the world have also been alerted.

Sixth: Under the Charter of the United Nations, we are asking tonight that an emergency meeting of the Security Council be convoked without delay to take action against this latest Soviet threat to world peace. Our resolution will call for the prompt dismantling and withdrawal of all offensive weapons in Cuba, under the supervision of U.N. observers, before the quarantine can be lifted.

Seventh and finally: I call upon Chairman Khrushchev to halt and eliminate this clandestine, reckless, and provocative threat to world peace and to stable relations between our two nations. I call upon him further to abandon this course of world domination, and to join in an historic effort to end the perilous arms race and to transform the history of man. He has an opportunity now to move the world back from the abyss of destruction by returning to his government's own words that it had no need to station missiles outside its own territory, and withdrawing these weapons from Cuba by refraining from any action which will widen or deepen the present crisis, and then by participating in a search for peaceful and permanent solutions.

This nation is prepared to present its case against the Soviet threat to peace, and our own proposals for a peaceful world, at any time and in any forum—in the OAS, in the United Nations, or in any other meeting that could be useful—without limiting our freedom of action. We have in the past made strenuous efforts to limit the spread of nuclear weapons. We have proposed the elimination of all arms and military bases in a fair and effective disarmament treaty. We are prepared to discuss new proposals for the removal of tensions on both sides, including the possibilities of a genuinely independent Cuba, free to determine its own destiny. We have no wish to war with the Soviet Union—for we are a peaceful people who desire to live in peace with all other peoples.

But it is difficult to settle or even discuss these problems in an atmosphere of intimidation. That is why this latest Soviet threat—or any other threat which is made either independently or in response to our actions this week—must and will be met with determination. Any hostile move anywhere in the world against the safety and freedom of peoples to whom we are committed, including in particular the brave people of West Berlin, will be met by whatever action is needed.

Finally, I want to say a few words to the captive people of Cuba, to whom this speech is being directly carried by special radio facilities.

I speak to you as a friend, as one who knows of your deep attachment to your fatherland, as one who shares your aspirations for liberty and justice for all. And I have watched and the American people have watched with deep sorrow how your nationalist revolution was betrayed—and how your fatherland fell under foreign domination. Now your leaders are no longer Cuban leaders inspired by Cuban ideals. They are puppets and agents of an international conspiracy which has turned Cuba against your friends and neighbors in the Americas, and turned it into the first Latin American country to become a target for nuclear war— the first Latin American country to have these weapons on its soil.

These new weapons are not in your interest. They contribute nothing to your peace and well-being. They can only undermine it. But this country has no wish to cause you to suffer or to impose any system upon you. We know that your lives and land are being used as pawns by those who deny your freedom. Many times in the past, the Cuban people have risen to throw out tyrants who destroyed their liberty. And I have no doubt that most Cubans today look forward to the time when they will be truly free—free from foreign domination, free to choose their own leaders, free to select their own system, free to own their own land, free to speak and write and worship without fear or degradation. And then shall Cuba be welcomed back to the society of free nations and to the associations of this hemisphere.

My fellow citizens, let no one doubt that this is a difficult and dangerous effort on which we have set out. No one can foresee precisely what course it will take or what costs or casualties will be incurred. Many months of sacrifice and self-discipline lie ahead—months in which both our patience and our will will be tested, months in which many threats and denunciations will keep us aware of our dangers. But the greatest danger of all would be to do nothing.

The path we have chosen for the present is full of hazards, as all paths are; but it is the one most consistent with our character and courage as a nation and our commitments around the world. The cost of freedom is always high, but Americans have always paid it. And one path we shall never choose, and that is the path of surrender or submission.

Our goal is not the victory of might, but the vindication of right; not peace at the expense of freedom, but both peace and freedom, here in this hemisphere, and, we hope, around the world. God willing, that goal will be achieved.

Thank you and good night.

Ronald Reagan

Remarks at the Brandenburg Gate

delivered 12 June 1987, West Berlin

Retrieved from http://www.americanrhetoric.com/speeches/fdrarsenalof democracy.html. American Rhetoric: Top 100 Speeches

[AUTHENTICITY CERTIFIED: Text version below
transcribed directly from audio. (2)]

Thank you. Thank you, very much.

Chancellor Kohl, Governing Mayor Diepgen, ladies and gentlemen: Twenty-four years ago, President John F. Kennedy visited Berlin, and speaking to the people of this city and the world at the city hall. Well since then two other presidents have come, each in his turn to Berlin. And today, I, myself, make my second visit to your city.

We come to Berlin, we American Presidents, because it's our duty to speak in this place of freedom. But I must confess, we're drawn here by other things as well; by the feeling of history in this city—more than 500 years older than our own nation; by the beauty of the Grunewald and the Tiergarten; most of all, by your courage and determination. Perhaps the composer, Paul Linke, understood something about American Presidents. You see, like so many Presidents before me, I come here today because wherever I go, whatever I do: "Ich hab noch einen Koffer in Berlin." [I still have a suitcase in Berlin.]

Our gathering today is being broadcast throughout Western Europe and North America. I understand that it is being seen and heard as well in the East. To those listening throughout Eastern Europe, I extend my warmest greetings and the good will of the American people. To those listening in East Berlin, a special word: Although I cannot be with you, I address my remarks to you just as surely as to those standing here before me. For I join you, as I join your fellow countrymen in the West, in this firm, this unalterable belief: Es gibt nur ein Berlin. [There is only one Berlin.]

Behind me stands a wall that encircles the free sectors of this city, part of a vast system of barriers that divides the entire continent of Europe. From the Baltic South, those barriers cut across Germany in a gash of barbed wire, concrete, dog runs, and guard towers. Farther south, there may be no visible, no obvious wall. But there remain armed guards and checkpoints all the same—still a restriction on the right to travel, still an instrument to impose upon ordinary men and women the will of a totalitarian state.

Yet, it is here in Berlin where the wall emerges most clearly; here, cutting across your city, where the news photo and the television screen have imprinted this brutal division of a continent upon the mind of the world.

Standing before the Brandenburg Gate, every man is a German separated from his fellow men.

Every man is a Berliner, forced to look upon a scar.

President Von Weizsäcker has said, "The German question is open as long as the Brandenburg Gate is closed." Well today—today I say: As long as this gate is closed, as long as this scar of a wall is permitted to stand, it is not the German question alone that remains open, but the question of freedom for all mankind.

Yet, I do not come here to lament. For I find in Berlin a message of hope, even in the shadow of this wall, a message of triumph.

In this season of spring in 1945, the people of Berlin emerged from their air-raid shelters to find devastation. Thousands of miles away, the people of the United States reached out to help. And in 1947 Secretary of State—as you've been told—George Marshall announced the creation of what would become known as the Marshall Plan. Speaking precisely 40 years ago this month, he said: "Our policy is directed not against any country or doctrine, but against hunger, poverty, desperation, and chaos."

In the Reichstag a few moments ago, I saw a display commemorating this 40th anniversary of the Marshall Plan. I was struck by a sign—the sign on a burnt-out, gutted structure that was being rebuilt. I understand that Berliners of my own generation can remember seeing signs like it dotted throughout the western sectors of the city. The sign read simply: "The Marshall Plan is helping here to strengthen the free world." A strong, free world in the West—that dream became real. Japan rose from ruin to become an economic giant. Italy, France, Belgium— virtually every nation in Western Europe saw political and economic rebirth; the European Community was founded.

In West Germany and here in Berlin, there took place an economic miracle, the Wirtschaftswunder. Adenauer, Erhard, Reuter, and other leaders understood the practical importance of liberty—that just as truth can flourish only when the journalist is given freedom of speech, so prosperity can come about only when the farmer and businessman enjoy economic freedom. The German leaders—the German leaders reduced tariffs, expanded free trade, lowered taxes. From 1950 to 1960 alone, the standard of living in West Germany and Berlin doubled.

Where four decades ago there was rubble, today in West Berlin there is the greatest industrial output of any city in Germany: busy office blocks, fine homes and apartments, proud avenues, and the spreading lawns of parkland. Where a city's culture seemed to have been destroyed, today there are two great universities, orchestras and an opera, countless theaters, and museums. Where there was want, today there's abundance—food, clothing, automobiles—the wonderful goods of the Kudamm. From devastation, from utter ruin, you Berliners have, in freedom, rebuilt a city that once again ranks as one of the greatest on earth. Now the Soviets may have had other plans. But my friends, there were a few things the Soviets didn't count on: Berliner Herz, Berliner Humor, ja, und Berliner Schnauze. [Berliner heart, Berliner humor, yes, and a Berliner Schnauze.]

In the 1950s—in the 1950s Khrushchev predicted: "We will bury you."

But in the West today, we see a free world that has achieved a level of prosperity and well-being unprecedented in all human history. In the Communist world, we see failure, technological backwardness, declining standards of health, even want of the most basic kind—too little food. Even today, the Soviet Union still cannot feed itself. After these four decades, then, there stands before the entire world one great and inescapable conclusion: freedom leads to prosperity. Freedom replaces the ancient hatreds among the nations with comity and peace. Freedom is the victor.

And now—now the Soviets themselves may, in a limited way, be coming to understand the importance of freedom. We hear much from Moscow about a new policy of reform and openness. Some political prisoners have been released. Certain foreign news broadcasts are no longer being jammed. Some economic enterprises have been permitted to operate with greater freedom from state control.

Are these the beginnings of profound changes in the Soviet state? Or are they token gestures intended to raise false hopes in the West, or to strengthen the Soviet system without changing it? We welcome change and openness; for we believe that freedom and security go together, that the advance of human liberty—the advance of human liberty can only strengthen the cause of world peace.

There is one sign the Soviets can make that would be unmistakable, that would advance dramatically the cause of freedom and peace.

General Secretary Gorbachev, if you seek peace, if you seek prosperity for the Soviet Union and Eastern Europe, if you seek liberalization: come here to this gate.

Mr. Gorbachev, open this gate.

Mr. Gorbachev—Mr. Gorbachev, tear down this wall!

I understand the fear of war and the pain of division that afflict this continent, and I pledge to you my country's efforts to help overcome these burdens. To be sure, we in the West must resist Soviet expansion. So, we must maintain defenses of unassailable strength. Yet we seek peace; so we must strive to reduce arms on both sides.

Beginning 10 years ago, the Soviets challenged the Western alliance with a grave new threat, hundreds of new and more deadly SS-20 nuclear missiles capable of striking every capital in Europe. The Western alliance responded by committing itself to a counter-deployment (unless the Soviets agreed to negotiate a better solution)—namely, the elimination of such weapons on both sides. For many months, the Soviets refused to bargain in earnestness. As the alliance, in turn, prepared to go forward with its counter-deployment, there were difficult days, days of protests like those during my 1982 visit to this city; and the Soviets later walked away from the table.

But through it all, the alliance held firm. And I invite those who protested then—I invite those who protest today—to mark this fact: because we remained strong, the Soviets came back to the table. Because we remained strong, today we have within reach the possibility, not merely of limiting the growth of arms, but of eliminating, for the first time, an entire class of nuclear weapons from the face of the earth.

As I speak, NATO ministers are meeting in Iceland to review the progress of our proposals for eliminating these weapons. At the talks in Geneva, we have also proposed deep cuts in strategic offensive weapons. And the Western allies have likewise made far-reaching proposals to reduce the danger of conventional war and to place a total ban on chemical weapons.

While we pursue these arms reductions, I pledge to you that we will maintain the capacity to deter Soviet aggression at any level at which it might occur. And in cooperation with many of our allies, the United States is pursuing the Strategic Defense Initiative—research to base deterrence not on the threat of offensive retaliation, but on defenses that truly defend; on systems, in short, that will not target populations, but shield them. By these means we seek to increase the safety of Europe and all the world. But we must remember a crucial fact: East and West do not mistrust each other because we are armed; we are armed because we mistrust each other. And our differences are not about weapons but about liberty. When President Kennedy spoke at the City Hall those 24 years ago, freedom was encircled; Berlin was under siege. And today, despite all the pressures upon this city, Berlin stands secure in its liberty. And freedom itself is transforming the globe.

In the Philippines, in South and Central America, democracy has been given a rebirth. Throughout the Pacific, free markets are working miracle after miracle of economic growth. In the industrialized nations, a technological revolution is taking place, a revolution marked by rapid, dramatic advances in computers and telecommunications.

In Europe, only one nation and those it controls refuse to join the community of freedom. Yet in this age of redoubled economic growth, of information and innovation, the Soviet Union faces a choice: it must make fundamental changes, or it will become obsolete.

Today, thus, represents a moment of hope. We in the West stand ready to cooperate with the East to promote true openness, to break down barriers that separate people, to create a safer, freer world. And surely there is no better place than Berlin, the meeting place of East and West, to make a start.

Free people of Berlin: today, as in the past, the United States stands for the strict observance and full implementation of all parts of the Four Power Agreement of 1971. Let us use this occasion, the 750th anniversary of this city, to usher in a new era, to seek a still fuller, richer life for the Berlin of the future. Together, let us maintain and develop the ties between the Federal Republic and the Western sectors of Berlin, which is permitted by the 1971 agreement.

And I invite Mr. Gorbachev: let us work to bring the Eastern and Western parts of the city closer together, so that all the inhabitants of all Berlin can enjoy the benefits that come with life in one of the great cities of the world.

To open Berlin still further to all Europe, East and West, let us expand the vital air access to this city, finding ways of making commercial air service to Berlin more convenient, more comfortable, and more economical. We look to the day when West Berlin can become one of the chief aviation hubs in all central Europe.

With—with our French—with our French and British partners, the United States is prepared to help bring international meetings to Berlin. It would be only fitting for Berlin to serve as the site of United Nations meetings, or world conferences on human rights and arms control, or other issues that call for international cooperation.

There is no better way to establish hope for the future than to enlighten young minds, and we would be honored to sponsor summer youth exchanges, cultural events, and other programs for young Berliners from the East. Our French and British friends, I'm certain, will do the same. And it's my hope that an authority can be found in East Berlin to sponsor visits from young people of the Western sectors.

One final proposal, one close to my heart: Sport represents a source of enjoyment and ennoblement, and you may have noted that the Republic of Korea—South Korea—has offered to permit certain events of the 1988 Olympics to take place in the North. International sports competitions of all kinds could take place in both parts of this city. And what better way to demonstrate to the world the openness of this city than to offer in some future year to hold the Olympic games here in Berlin, East and West.

In these four decades, as I have said, you Berliners have built a great city. You've done so in spite of threats—the Soviet attempts to impose the East-mark, the blockade. Today the city thrives in spite of the challenges implicit in the very presence of this wall. What keeps you here? Certainly there's a great deal to be said for your fortitude, for your defiant courage. But I believe there's something deeper, something that involves Berlin's whole look and feel and way of life—not mere sentiment. No one could live long in Berlin without being completely disabused of illusions. Something, instead, that has seen the difficulties of life in Berlin but chose to accept them, that continues to build this good and proud city in contrast to a surrounding totalitarian presence, that refuses to release human energies or aspirations, something that speaks with a powerful voice of affirmation, that says "yes" to this city, yes to the future, yes to freedom. In a word, I would submit that what keeps you in Berlin—is "love."

Love both profound and abiding.

Perhaps this gets to the root of the matter, to the most fundamental distinction of all between East and West. The totalitarian world produces backwardness because it does such violence to the spirit, thwarting the human impulse to create, to enjoy, to worship. The totalitarian world finds even symbols of love and of worship an affront.

Years ago, before the East Germans began rebuilding their churches, they erected a secular structure: the television tower at Alexander Platz. Virtually ever since, the authorities have been working to correct what they view as the tower's one major flaw: treating the glass sphere at the top with paints and chemicals of every kind. Yet even today when the sun strikes that sphere, that sphere that towers over all Berlin, the light makes the sign of the cross. There in Berlin, like the city itself, symbols of love, symbols of worship, cannot be suppressed.

As I looked out a moment ago from the Reichstag, that embodiment of German unity, I noticed words crudely spray-painted upon the wall, perhaps by a young Berliner (quote):

"This wall will fall. Beliefs become reality."

Yes, across Europe, this wall will fall, for it cannot withstand faith; it cannot withstand truth. The wall cannot withstand freedom.

And I would like, before I close, to say one word. I have read, and I have been questioned since I've been here about certain demonstrations against my coming. And I would like to say just one thing, and to those who demonstrate so. I wonder if they have ever asked themselves that if they should have the kind of government they apparently seek, no one would ever be able to do what they're doing again.

Thank you and God bless you all. Thank you.

9 Persuasion, Perception, and the Law

Attorneys present persuasive messages in various forms in the course of their regular work. Indeed, much about law and litigation revolves around making a persuasive case to influence someone else's perception of a case and applicable laws, be it a judge, jury, or someone with whom one is negotiating an issue. Some of this work occurs privately via personal communication such as e-mail, and some of it occurs more publicly through submitted court documents and news reports in which attorneys provide information about the case and their own client's position on the case. This work also occurs in face-to-face meetings with each other, their clients, and in face-to-face presentation before a judge or jury. In all situations, the attorney must be aware of the means available to present the message as well as the audiences involved.

A growing body of scholarship on the neural attributes of persuasion in court cases and other legal settings exists (Freeman, 2011). For example, Capraro (2011) notes that when a powerful image is integrated to elicit emotional response, it usually has the intended effect (p. 414). While I have read some of this scholarship, I do not pretend to have legal training. My reports and analyses are based on observation, experience, a cursory understanding of legal studies, and mostly on principles of rhetoric.

In this chapter I present two legal case studies to illustrate application of the model in such situations. I use public information available; so, all of the case details that I present and related video to which I refer can be viewed by the reader for verification. One case involves debate about whether to pursue a trial related to a personal injury case. The other involves the arguments associated with the O.J. Simpson trial from 1995 regarding a glove as evidence in his murder trial.

Personal Injury Case—Avoid Court Litigation

Another kind of persuasive message one may encounter is litigation over a personal injury. I alluded in another chapter to a personal injury attorney and how he integrates narrative of his own injury in multimodal ways in advertising. I sustained an injury some years ago as a passenger in a vehicle. I will not detail what happened in the accident, but I will explain the pre-trial mediation I experienced and the persuasion associated with avoiding a trial. I am not an attorney; so, I do not know details of the processes they took to prepare for the mediation meeting. I respect their expertise in preparing for it and facilitating mediation.

Description

I sustained multiple injuries as the result of a vehicle accident. The insurance company involved never challenged the fault of the other driver, and my attorney maintained my medical records and treatments from the injuries. At some point after my condition was improving and an economic settlement was being negotiated I was asked to attend a pre-trial mediation session.

The session would include my attorneys, an attorney representing the other driver's insurance carrier, and a mediator who was also a legal professional, having practiced law in a few different positions. Settlement figures would be exchanged and discussed; however, it also represented an opportunity for the attorneys to assess whether it would be worthwhile to pursue a trial if the settlement figures were not satisfactory. I understood that the final decision would be my own, but the mediator and my attorneys would help me with an informed decision. If I wanted to pursue a trial I could and my attorneys would continue to represent me.

Dress Code

All five of us who attended the meeting, including me, were dressed nicely—all were male and dressed in some kind of business suit including a tie. So, there was an air of general respectfulness and professionalism about the room and exchange. All of us are well educated and articulate. So, the appearance of the exchanges seemed one of reason and professionalism.

Vocal Tone

There was no yelling involved at any time. We all seemed to understand this was a mediation session at which each side would present its case and look to the mediator for objectivity in assessing reasonableness. The volume was a normal conversational volume, as if it were a group of professionals discussing something serious.

Between the dress and vocal tone, my mirror neurons were engaged; I looked and seemed to behave as the attorneys did. My educational background compared well to theirs as well.

Prior Experience

Several years prior to this accident, I was involved in another accident that resulted in whiplash. I had done some research on normal factors involved in awarding a settlement based on the sum of the related medical bills. So, I had an idea of what may be considered reasonable. Beyond that experience, I had never had a legal experience beyond paying traffic fines without making a court appearance.

I respected that my attorneys were well educated in the law, and I respected that the mediator also was well trained and experienced. I trusted that they would not try to take advantage of me. I understood the insurance company representative was representing the other side and would try to negotiate within his company's interests.

My reward neurons were engaged at the prospect of a settlement, having an idea of what it may be, based on memories stored in my hippocampus of that previous experience.

Visual Dominance and Intermodal Sensory Redundancy

The dress and tone re-enforced the professional atmosphere. I perceived all were doing their job. We were all cleanly shaven, too. Again, this all gave the appearance that it was a meeting of well-educated and reasonable professionals.

Modal Filtering

Since everyone was dressed similarly and maintained a polite, professional tone, the focus was able to be on the messages and their reasonableness. My attorneys presented my case, and the other attorney listened. In fact, I do not recall him saying much at all. He had to make a few phone calls to his supervisors at some point, which took a couple of hours. However, when all returned, the mediator explained how reasonable his offer was. My attorneys re-enforced that assessment; this represents another kind of intermodal sensory redundancy—two sets of people, dressed as professionals in this setting, re-enforcing a message.

The mediator's message was that it was very close to an award provided in a trial of a similar case. He also acknowledged that a jury of people in that county may have not felt terribly sorry for me because of my profession. They would hear of my salary, and they may question giving more money to me. One of the jobs of an attorney is to understand the demographics of the county in which he or she practices; so that he or she could anticipate an outcome at trial. So, I appreciated that information, and it affected a decision.

Cognition: Perception and Decision

I decided to accept the amount offered. The mediator's observations that the amount was consistent with a jury award and that a jury may not give more money influenced me considerably. I also asked my attorneys their perception of the offer, and both agreed it was reasonable. So, my perception was that it would be reasonable, and I decided to accept it rather than go to trial.

O.J. Simpson: The Gloves

Description of Case

In 1994, O.J. Simpson, a former star football player and actor, was charged with murder of his wife and a friend of hers. It was considered among "the trials of the century" since it featured such a prominent person. During the course of the several month trial, the prosecution placed several items of evidence in front of the jury to consider in assessing Mr. Simpson's innocence or guilt. One of these was black leather gloves that had blood on them and that were found at Mr. Simpson's home. Testimony about the gloves can be found on YouTube (IbHmc Clannad Man, 2008).

Attorney Claims and Use of Gloves as Evidence

The prosecution asserted that Mr. Simpson wore the gloves in committing the crimes. The defense claimed he did not commit the crimes. The prosecution introduced the gloves as evidence, pointing to them having Simpson's DNA on it, as well as that of the victims; but the prosecution considered not having Simpson try the gloves on because the gloves had been soaked in blood and frozen and dried a few times.

The defense reviewed the gloves as evidence and challenged the prosecution to have Simpson try them on to see if they actually fit him. Eventually, the prosecution asked Simpson to try them on. In a famous scene of the trial, he tried them on and it was discovered that the gloves were much too small for him to have worn. After the incident, one of the prosecutors conveyed concern to the judge that Simpson, who had arthritis, had not taken medication for a few days, which could have lead his hands to swell. Also, Simpson wore a pair of white latex gloves when he tried on the black gloves; this also would have caused the gloves to seem a bit tight, contributing to the difficulty he had putting them on.

Analysis

I analyze the argument posited by the defense once the gloves were shown not to fit Mr. Simpson within the model's parameters to show how an audience likely perceived the assertion that Simpson wore them in committing the murders. Much of the audience's perception is affected by elements associated with Visual dominance and prior experience. The model appears below.

Visual Dominance

The episode occurred in a courtroom where testimony was given to a jury. Much of the trial was also broadcasted to a television audience live, and video of the effort to put the gloves on exists at YouTube. The jury and any others watching the scene could clearly see that Mr. Simpson was having considerable difficulty putting the gloves on. If he had in fact worn the gloves, as the prosecution asserted, they should have gone on relatively easily, even with the latex gloves on. One could assume some difficulty given the latex gloves, but Simpson should have been able to put them on much more easily than he did. The image of his struggle to put on the gloves and very awkward appearance once they were on as far as they could go on could only mean that the gloves truly did not fit at all in the first place.

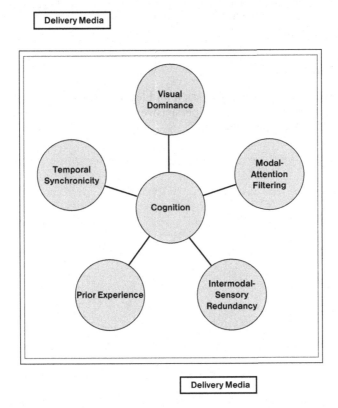

Figure 9.1 Model.

Prior Experience

An audience could draw from their own experience with tight gloves that one who struggled so much with a pair of gloves likely could never have worn them at all, much less in committing murder. So, the prior experience attribute helps the visual dominance attribute's dynamic as well. Many people have either experienced such a struggle themselves or witnessed a similar struggle involving a friend or relative. Memories in one's hippocampus of such an experience would explain the visual image of Simpson's struggle with these gloves.

Temporal Synchronicity

There is a question about the connection between Simpson and the gloves; the gloves were bloodied and the prosecution has asserted their involvement in the murders. The audience is aware of those assertions before Simpson attempts to put them on. Yet, when he tries to put them on and struggles so much to do so, the initial verbal assertion is contradicted dramatically by the image of the struggle. Through these, the audience perceives/concludes that the gloves and Simpson are not connected (Cognition).

Conclusion

These two cases involving litigation and legal maneuvering illustrate the application of the model to the persuasive messages attorneys present on a regular basis in their work.

10 Applications in Production of Materials

The previous chapters considered analysis of messages in various forms after the materials were produced. That is, I presented the reader with a description of a multimodal message and then showed an analysis that included neuroscientific concepts and the model I have proposed. The reader may say to him or herself, "that's all well and good, but how do I apply this to something I have to develop for work or an assignment at school?" In this chapter I attempt to facilitate an understanding of how to apply this model in the production of multimodal persuasive materials. I present three cases and how one can think about these concepts toward producing multimodal persuasive messages. Two cases involve a school levy issue: one in a wealthy district and one in a lower middle class community. The third case involves a criminal law suit associated with a police shooting. I use these, because they demonstrate situations in which persuasion is challenging and always multimodal.

I cannot guarantee that the messages described here will be effective in persuading all members of a given audience, though. As stated back in Chapter 1, rhetoric is an art that may be based on understandings of various sciences associated with the audience. The smaller the audience the easier it is to persuade them. An audience of one is easiest to persuade because one can learn as much as one can about that person and what will influence him or her to make a certain decision. A larger audience, even of five people, is much more challenging to persuade, though. The number of various elements that would influence the group to agree on a single message increases exponentially compared to the audience of one person.

As I did in the previous chapter, I also offer a disclaimer. I have some background with marketing for non-profit organizations, but I am not involved in the discussions of either school district described here. I, also, am not an attorney; I have read some material pertaining to neuroscience and legal studies and base my analyses and suggestions on the combination of that material and my background with multimodal rhetoric scholarship and practice.

School Levies

I presented a few examples of political advertising in previous chapters. Campaigns tend to revolve around how the candidate or issue/new policy/legislation related to it can benefit the community. Mirror neurons and reward neurons are frequently engaged to appeal to the electorate; people the voters know and who are generally trustworthy are often used (mirror neurons), and the message generally indicates how the public will benefit (reward neurons). School levies are a common feature of election season. Generally, even in wealthy districts that can afford the levy passage, the appeal revolves around improving the learning experience for students somehow, thus benefitting the community. The benefits of having a strong school district to the community typically include higher property values and access to good colleges and, consequently, better education and good paying jobs, for students. So, these are among the appeals to reward neurons—everyone benefits, even those without children in the school district (higher property values).

For the most part, the argument against a levy revolves around the need for the levy ("how much will not passing the levy negatively affect students and property values? We are doing very well now; so, how bad can it get if we wait a few years to pass another levy?") and the use of funds raised by the levy ("I don't want my taxes wasted!"). These are valid concerns, and counterarguments can emphasize how it is important to maintain excellent standards so that there is no decline in student academic performance, and how waiting to pass a levy will only make the next levy that much higher and more important to pass. It is better to pass levies periodically on a small scale/increase than to wait to have to pass a larger levy all at once. As for the wastefulness of a levy's use, that counterargument would need to show how current funds are not wasted, reassuring the electorate that future funds will also not be wasted.

However, what happens if the citizens of the district cannot afford passage of a levy because it would raise property taxes when the economy of the district is already stressed? This presents a very different situation than considered within a wealthy district. People may agree that a good education is important and levy funds would probably be used well. However, the economic stress that the majority of people in the district face negatively influence the outcome. I have actually seen a letter to the editor of a local newspaper claim, in effect, that, "A good school district is bad because it results in increased property taxes" (my own paraphrase of the message). The extended message followed this logic: 1) increasing property taxes is generally bad; 2) increasing property taxes to fund a school levy may result in improving the school's performance, which will 3) cause property values in the school district to increase, thereby 4) resulting in even higher property taxes. So, a weak-performing school district is preferable to a good one.

The challenge is not limited to communities struggling economically. What of those citizens who generally disapprove of high taxes no matter the economy? What of those who perceive, based on data, that the district is performing very well and should not need more money? Even strong school districts may need to develop a persuasive message to encourage voters to pass a levy.

Because of these differing situations relative to a single issue—school levy, I provide a means by which to develop materials to promote passage of a levy in each situation and using the model. School levy messages are generally in the form of print-linguistic signage on lawns; however, images can be added. Also, the message can be presented through video. I use both methods here. I am not presently involved as a consultant in either district; though, I live in the county in which both are located. I use information available to the general public from online sites and through news media. Finally, the scenario described is based on a recently-passed bi-annual state budget; though, the legislature is attempting to address a cut in funds to certain districts. The state budget provided more funding to school districts that had an average home value under a certain amount and cut funding to districts that had an average home value above that amount. As of the writing of this chapter, the state is easing some of the initial restrictions it imposed. As in the previous chapters, I provide the illustration of the model below.

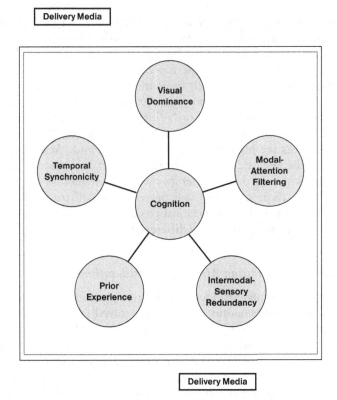

Figure 10.1 Model.

Upper Middle Class District

Description

Periodically, a school district that is doing well academically and has wealth in it asks citizens to pass a levy because it needs additional funds to purchase newer instructional materials and technologies to maintain its excellent programs. One such district that had state funding cut because of its economic position discussed pursuing a school levy to make up some of that funding loss only one year after it had passed a levy. The state legislature had passed a budget that redistributed funds for public education such that districts that had a median household value above a certain amount ($210,000 is an approximation) would get less funding from the state because they could afford to pass levies to support education more than districts that had a median home value below that amount could. Those economically challenged districts would receive additional funding to help them overcome challenges of passing levies. The median household value in this district was over $230,000, and the median household income was almost $80,000 (all dollar figures in this section are based on data from 2013)—both well above the national median household value and household income levels (www.city-data.com/city/a [note: I use "a" and "b" in the citation to maintain each district's anonymity]).

The school district itself is the best performing district in the particular county, ranking among the top-20 within the state in academic performance relative to over 20 measures. It had maintained that approximate ranking over the previous 10 years. It routinely was rated as "Excellent with distinction" or "A" (the state rating system changed a few times over the course of the period considered; "Excellent with distinction" was the highest rating of 6 possible, and "Academic Emergency" was the lowest). Residents of this district had passed the earlier levy without knowing that another levy would be requested so soon after. So, a challenge to pass the levy was presented: the district is doing very well academically and a levy was just passed. The appeal would be that the district needs to make up the difference to ensure continued success.

Local Economic Situation Affecting Considerations

The biggest developments locally over the previous three years that affect political and economic dynamics involved in the levy argument include plans to develop a particular area as residential/commercial/industrial and potential increase in population related to that. There is already a good commercial and industrial base, and real estate taxes, consequently, are not terribly high. In many wealthy areas that have little commerce or industry in them, taxes tend to be very high to cover the lack of those items; however, those residents tend to like having less industry in their area. There was also some backlash related to closing a golf course that was no longer profitable and was purchased by the city a few years prior. It has been converted to a park.

According to demographic data available publicly online, the city has a strong professional population and a median age of 46 years (www.city-data.com/city/a). So, many are established professionals. An interesting piece of data is that the average stay of people once they move in is below the state average, suggesting that many live there for a while but then move out. This could be connected to the school district's success; residents may move to the district as their children reach school age and stay throughout that period, then move out. However, if this is the case, then it should be considered within the development of materials for a levy.

Historical Strengths of District

I attempt to identify historical strengths, because these can be used in promotional materials. As mentioned above, historically the district has performed very well academically. Many of its students go on to college, some at highly respected private institutions. The district has experienced periods of growth through housing developments spread over several decades, and that will continue.

Promotional Materials

I describe some attributes of each promotional tool that should be integrated. I describe a flyer that would be not more than a tri-fold 8 ½" by 11". I also describe the content of a five-eight-minute video to be placed on the district's website and promoted through the flyer.

Flyer

A flyer promoting the levy's passage should integrate information about the historical performance of the district and how property taxes in the district are still relatively low compared to other districts. A nearby district, for example, that is also considered wealthy and tends to perform as well as this district has very high property taxes. This point should be explicitly stated.

Images of students who graduated and have gone on to prestigious colleges can also be included—these would engage reward neurons as well as mirror neurons. Voters who have attended college recognize the value of that education, and they would want their children to mirror those graduates' success. Such images should be of students who were recognized locally; so, there is some immediate recollection of them. There may even be a testimonial (narrative) from a student indicating the impact their education at the district had in helping them succeed. These students should be nicely dressed, to elicit mirror neurons recalling good, disciplined students.

Video

Likewise, a video promoting the levy should be developed integrating many of the same messages and materials. The superintendent may act as the primary spokesperson, dressed professionally, providing information about the performance and status of the district, while an image of the data itself is visible. A couple of former and current students could provide narratives about their experiences as well, showing images of them in district classrooms or at college. One may even be from a recent college graduate who has a very good job (long term reward).

The biggest challenge for this district is helping voters understand the need to raise funds to replace state funds. That should be part of the message as well; "it isn't our fault and the state believes we can raise the funds needed, making us more independent from state support."

Recognizing the need to limit intermodal interference, the screen should not show more than one person and one school building behind him or her at a time. It may also show just text and the image of a building alternatively.

Lower Middle Class District

Description

Another school district within a 20-minute drive of the wealthy district also had a challenge to pass a levy. Even though it benefitted from the additional state funding, it had not passed a levy in over 10 years. Before the state had passed the new budget helping poorer districts, the amount of the levy requests in this district had grown by 4 mills over the 4 years of trying. The last time the levy was presented to voters prior to this situation it was actually presented as two separate levies—one an instructional materials and equipment levy and the other a building and facilities maintenance levy. Each was valued at about the same number of mills; but voters could choose one, both, or none. They chose not to pass either. The median household value in this district was $100,000, and the median household income was $35,000—both below the national medians (www.city-data.com/city/b).

The school district itself was ranked among the lower half, at the border with the lower third, of schools academically in the state. Less than ten years prior it had been rated an "excellent" district, placing it in the top one third in the state; its ranking had declined over the next five years to "effective" and then "continuous improvement" or "C."

Local Economic Situation Affecting Considerations

There is a large manufacturing jobs base in this city, and as those jobs have declined so too has the local economy and employment. About ten years prior to this writing, the state provided funding to help the district build a new high school; however, other buildings in the district are older than 40 years and are falling into disrepair. There was an effort to revitalize the downtown area—in the city's historic center—that involved restoring and upgrading a few commercial buildings that also have apartments in upper floors. Those floors in at least one building were designated as housing for mentally ill persons receiving federal assistance. There are several federally-funded programs within the city that seem to comprise some portion of the city's economy. There are no plans for residential housing development; though, there is a government-banking program to motivate residents to improve their homes—low interest rate financing on home improvements.

Interestingly, the unemployment rate in this city is the same as that of the wealthy district's city; however, residents have jobs that provide lower incomes. Over 60% of the students in this district live in poverty. The median age is under 40 years; so, it is a younger population generally (www.city-data.com/city/b). This may be because of the affordability of housing; though, over 2/3 of housing in this city is rental property. While the wealthier district had a lower stay of residence once people moved in, the lower middle class city has a higher than average stay. This can suggest that people find the city appealing and stay longer; or, it means they are not able to move out to other cities—less mobile because of low incomes. Many of the teachers in the district have lived in the district all their life, having attended and graduated from the district. There is also a relatively large sector of retired residents who have lived in the city all of their lives. So, there is a strong local connection to the city; though, many are on fixed incomes or low incomes.

One may reasonably speculate that, because of the combination of the high rate of rental properties in the city and the high level of poverty among children in the school district (both over 60%), many of the rental units may be occupied by renters who receive federal support; so, they are on a fixed income. Consequently, there may be property owners who fear losing rental income with increased property taxes. The property tax they pay would increase, but the amount they could collect from rental fees would not increase. I posit this as a reasonable assumption, because the city has passed two income tax issues, increasing income taxes by .5% in just two years. So, citizens are willing to increase taxes, just not property taxes, evidently. This is phenomenon is of interest, further; because the city's income tax rate is among the highest in the state, while its property tax rate is a bit lower than that in most cities in the county. This complicates the dynamics involved in the situation generally, because property owners who rent may pressure renters who are not on a fixed income or who are unaware of fixed rent rules into voting against a levy they would, otherwise, support.

Historical Strengths of District

The district has performed well academically at different periods of time. Prior to the most recent levy passage (about ten years prior) the district was struggling relative to state standardized test results. However, within three years of passing the levy, as mentioned above, it was rated "excellent." Also, some graduates of the district have gone on to graduate from college and hold prestigious jobs. A 19th-century U.S. Supreme Court justice came from the district; a more recent graduate (1980s) is a district judge. Others have become physicians or attorneys.

The district generally has a very strong athletic presence in the county in which it competes. The football team has competed in the state play-offs several times in the past ten years, for example.

Promotional Materials

Flyer

A flyer should contain reminders about the historical successes the district has had, including a reference to the previous levy passage and resulting impact on performance. It should also contain references to how student academic success impacts local businesses; many students work part time within the local business environment or may graduate and eventually be employed there; the customer experience is better when employees with which the public interacts are well educated. All of these points should attempt to show the direct and indirect value of a good education.

Images on the flyer should include the new high school as well as an older building that is falling into disrepair. These will help voters who are not as engaged with the buildings understand the need for the monies raised. It should also explicitly mention the success linked to the previous levy passage—engaging reward neurons.

Colors should be bright to elicit positive emotions; the image of the building that is in disrepair can be in black and white, re-enforcing the negative image.

Video

Likewise, a video should include the superintendent as primary spokesperson, dressed professionally, talking about these items while images show the buildings in various condition. Current students can be used as well, talking about how better resources could help them perform better. One may be a recent graduate attending college. That person's narrative should describe the success he or she was able to find in the district that prepared him or her for college. These would engage mirror and reward neurons while helping voters recall prior experiences with the district's success. Students shown should be dressed in nice sporty to casual wear to mirror the image of a good, disciplined student.

The video can include testimony, also, from a local business person or manager at the local grocer, talking about the quality of employees drawn from the students working there. This person should be dressed professionally relative to the acceptable dress code of their business/ profession. They should mirror adults in the community concerned about business matters and a favorable economic perception.

The video could also include a reference to the success of the sports teams while contrasting it with the declining academic performance, calling on voters to bring the academic performance to the level of athletic performance. That may appeal well with the athletically inclined voters.

As with the other school levy video, the screen should not show more than one person and one building behind him or her at a time. It may also show just text and the image of a building alternatively.

Renter-Related Caveat

Again, voter action may be influenced by a misperception of or misrepresentation regarding how property tax increases can affect renters who are on a fixed income. Consequently, part of the message, or a separate message, needs to include that information. A flier circulated to parents of students or billboards around the city can include such information. It can also include a message about the value of moderate increases in rental fee as part of a community effort to improve children's education, stimulating mirror neurons by drawing on the link to the community. An image of a respected senior citizen can be used to represent members of the community who are on a fixed income. Such an image carries with it a link to the city's history as well as a symbol of one on a fixed income. The image could include that person's grandchild, especially if he or she is a student in the district. Including the grandchild re-enforces a link between past and future, eliciting both mirror and reward neurons.

Tamir Rice Independent Investigation Report Arguments

As I indicated in a previous chapter, attorneys routinely develop persuasive messages dealing with cases with which they are involved. Legal cases, especially involving criminal activity, involve arguments over several items. A case that is still under investigation and has yet to be presented to the grand jury (as of the date of the writing of this chapter) involves a white police officer shooting a 12-year old African-American boy. I present analysis of a possible way of developing a persuasive message for both sides related to the debate over an investigation report that has drawn criticism from the defense team.

Description of Case

In November of 2014, police in Cleveland, Ohio received a 911 call from an observer who saw a male playing with a gun near a playground in a public recreation center. According to various reports, the person who called 911 indicated that the gun was probably "fake;" though, he never ascertained whether it was real or fake. This information was not provided to the police who responded. Two police officers in a single vehicle responded to the scene and immediately observed the male walking around a gazebo. They observed the male place a gun in his waistband, and as they pulled up to the immediate scene the male reached into his waistband. As the car slowed to a stop, but before it had stopped, one officer—Timothy Loehmann—shot the male twice in the torso at close range. The male—Tamir Rice—died the next day of his injuries.

The officer is White, and the male victim is African-American, and the shooting occurred within the context of a national debate about police shootings of African-Americans and unwarranted use of force. The case drew national attention in the United States because of this connection and the fact that the gun was fake. In effect, Mr. Rice was unarmed when the officer shot him. In addition to the "White officer—African American victim" dynamics, much of the debate and investigations following the shooting focused on how quickly Officer Loehmann used deadly force and the general inability to verify whether Rice's gun was real or fake. As of the writing of this chapter, an investigation resulted in no criminal charges being presented. Public debate about the incident continues and litigation involving a civil claim of wrongful death continues.

I present for analysis competing claims of the objectivity of a particular "independent" investigation report the prosecution in the criminal case sought and expected to present to the grand jury for consideration. The authors of the report have background in legal studies and police work, and they found that Officer Loehmann acted reasonably in the situation. Mr. Rice's family's attorney disputes their objectivity and challenged the report as "independent." Prosecutors responded to that claim by defending the report as independent and the authors as objective. These competing claims represent opposing perceptions of a single item that could be used in a trial or litigation, and attorneys provided their reasoning for their assertion. I analyze the claims and reasoning within the model's framework because attributes of the claims are supported by video of the shooting and video shortly before and after the shooting occurred. Various people have offered conflicting perceptions of what is happening in the videos. Generally, the officers claim that they ordered Rice three times to put his hands up after getting out of the car, but the video does not show that; officers claim they observed Rice reaching for a gun in his waistband and pulling it out before shooting him; the video shows him grabbing his shirt to show police the gun in his waistband; he is not holding a gun when he falls to the ground after being shot.

Report and Attorney Claims

Again, the report, based on several months of interviews and review of video evidence, found the officer's actions to be reasonable in that particular situation. The particular report was authored by Kimberly Crawford, a former FBI supervisor, and Lamar Sims, Senior Deputy District Attorney from Denver, Colorado. As the Rice family attorney, Subodh Chandra, states in an interview with news media, the two have a history of biased actions; and, consequently, their investigation cannot be considered independent or objective:

> Chandra cited an interview with Sims posted on YouTube and aired on Denver public access television back in May with Sims apparently giving comments on the Rice case.
>
> Chandra also commented on an opinion rendered by Crawford, in support of use of force by the FBI in the high profile 1992 shootings at Ruby Ridge that left three dead. The case was later denounced by the U.S. Justice Department and then FBI Director Louis Freeh as being "terribly flawed."
>
> Chandra believes with these types of backgrounds, Crawford and Sims are not able to make independent assessments of the Rice case.
>
> "One of them had a preconceived notion about the case already that he brought to the table," Chandra said. "And it appears that the other one has formed opinions in the past that even the U.S. Department of Justice has rejected as being outside of the law."
>
> Pagonakis, 2015

According to the same news report, the County prosecutor involved with the criminal investigation, Timothy McGinty, responded to the challenge by stating,

> "My staff was instructed to find and ask the nation's finest teachers and experienced professionals in the field of the use of deadly force by police to study the facts and render their opinion in light of the Supreme Court's instructions. Neither expert who has reported so far was financially motivated, and to my knowledge, they do not testify as part of their source of income. One has taught the subject

to the most professional law enforcement agency in our nation and perhaps the world: The FBI.

The other lawyer is also highly respected: An experienced lead prosecutor in Colorado who has taught the subject and is an author of the Denver DA's protocol on use of force which also promotes a high level of transparency.

This Prosecutor's Office's policy—requiring a high level of transparency in the investigations of deadly of force cases by police and giving the ultimate decision to the Grand Jury—will make police across the county more accountable and will reduce the number of unnecessary deaths of both civilians and police while increasing the public's confidence in its system of justice.

It has already produced significant policy reforms post-Brelo including a dramatic reduction in the number and length of high speed chases that endanger the public. The oversight of the Department of Justice with its specific goals will only underscore Cleveland's determination to improve its performance."

The reports will be given to a grand jury, which will consider criminal charges in the Rice case.

Pagonakis, 2015

McGinty's basic claim is that the two authors have a reputation as recognized experts and should be considered independent and objective.

Analysis

I identified the main message from each attorney in the previous section, and I analyze the claims here within the model's parameters to show how an audience could perceive the accuracy of the competing claims. The primary audience of both messages is the general public; the information is reported by the news media to the public using means available to the general public—print media, television, and the Internet. However, it is reasonable to anticipate a jury or judge becoming an audience.

Much of that audience's perception is affected by elements associated with prior experience, as noted in previous chapters. However, there is overlap with the other attributes of the model because videos related to the shooting exist.

Prior Experience

The potential audience has learned to respect police officers as representing law and security. The audience, also, understands that officers generally do not use deadly force unless provoked in a situation in which their life is threatened by someone else. However, the audience has also heard of cases in which unethical officers have abused their authority or used

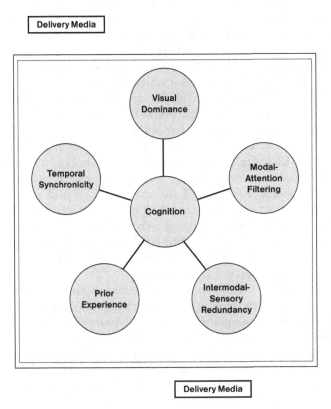

Figure 10.2 Model.

excessive force to address a given situation. I do not list any examples here; one needs only to Google "police use of excessive force" to find a listing of several examples. Some may have experience of having been mistreated, or with friends who were mistreated, by police. Finally, in the immediate context, the public is likely aware of the previous shootings of African Americans by White police officers since the debate was a national one and in the news for at least two years. So, one could be affected by either perspective relative to the case itself. The audience's perception of the case facts, prior to this debate about the report's findings, may influence perception of the messages here.

The perception of police as keepers of law and safety would alleviate any concerns of the amygdala; there is nothing to fear, and police protect the general public from harm. One who has been negatively affected by police violence or excessive force may have memories in their hippocampus that elicit fear from the amygdala, though. So, both perspectives may influence an audience based on their own experiences with police. The prosecution would re-enforce that perception, while the defense would highlight the potential for abuse of power and use of excessive force, eliciting fear from the amygdala and drawing on those particular cases.

Another attribute of prior experience is that both attorneys use the report's authors' records, or prior experiences, to support their claim. Each focuses on the authors' record that supports their own claim. Chandra draws on video posted to YouTube of one of the authors already having formed an opinion. Chandra would likely show that video in court (Visual Dominance) to support that claim.

Chandra also states that a judgement by the other author was found to be flawed. Chandra asserts that both are pro-police, rendering their opinions biased in favor of police. An audience that is aware of other cases when people were biased for any reason would perceive such statements as accurate, influencing their perception against the authors' credibility. "Clearly, these are people who have shown themselves to be biased in the past; they are likely biased in this case too," one might perceive. The video related to the one author along with the video of the shooting would reinforce that perception.

McGinty, on the other hand, notes that both are considered in the legal community to be experts and that neither was compensated in any way for their work, suggesting them to be independent and objective. An audience that understands that recognition from an entire field regarding expertise and objectivity in someone as a powerful builder of credibility would perceive that the authors are credible and can be objective. Neither has a stake in the outcome of the case; so, they can be independent; though both were linked to government offices. Further, that neither is receiving economic compensation of any kind enhances the perception that they are objective and independent. If they were being paid by the prosecutor's office for the investigation, there could be a perceived bias toward favoring an outcome that the prosecution wanted. The prosecutor could even call on them in a trial environment as expert testimony, eliciting mirror neurons form a jury or judge.

The audiences' prior experiences with bias and credibility affect their perception of who is likely to be more correct in their statement—Chandra or McGinty. The jury selection process may shed light on the potential bias/perceptions of the jury; questions pertaining to prior experiences with police and perception of police could reveal such biases. The way those in the jury pool dress and behave toward oral questions about these may also reveal bias toward a given perception of police.

Visual Dominance

While the statements are delivered via print-linguistic text through the media outlets, they would be shown to a jury or judge, and the authors may be called on to testify at trial. Attorneys have alluded to the video evidence associated with the case and related to the authors of the report. The general public has access to these videos a well. So, one can easily access videos and watch the statements and actions. This also contributes to intermodal sensory redundancy and modal filtering. The attorneys have alluded to particular items, helping to shape which modes the audience might choose to focus on—visual and/or print-linguistic. Again, if visual stimuli are present, the audience is likely to consider it heavily.

The prosecution would need to rely on the visual representation on the two report authors in court as respected experts and tone as they respond to questions. So, the prosecutor would likely emphasize the live visual representation over the recordings of the one author.

Temporal Synchronicity and Redundancy

A few inconsistencies between the video of the shooting and the police report of the incident have been identified by investigators. Attorneys would likely show both to re-enforce the lack of credibility of the report. Chandra, in fact, could reasonably show the video of the shooting just before showing the police report and challenge the audience to ascertain how the police report could be perceived as credible. This is relevant because the authors of the investigation report conclude that the officer involved is acting reasonably based on information from the video and the police report. Showing the two pieces of evidence in close temporal proximity would raise doubt from a jury or judge.

While the two pieces are not consistent with each other, the audience would be looking for redundancy, and the lack of it would contribute to the perception (cognition) that the police report is not credible. (Note: since the initial writing of this chapter, the criminal case was resolved without charges being filed. The city and family reached a financial settlement for a related civil lawsuit.)

Conclusion

In this chapter I have shown how one may use the model toward producing multimodal persuasive messages, specifically in flyers, video, and in person. In the previous chapters, focus and analyses were relative to an existing message. So, this chapter provides examples of how to design materials using the model.

11 A Neurorhetorical Analysis of a Multimodal Print Persuasive Message

This text has been about the neuroscience of multimodal persuasive messages, which tends to be perceived as a message that integrates print, visual (beyond print text), and/or aural attributes. I have, also, integrated some examples that integrated spatial attributes of body or behavior such as speeches or face-to-face interactions. However, recognizing the importance of understanding both print-linguistic rhetoric as well as multimodal rhetoric, I include this chapter to illustrate application of a number of elements of the model presented throughout this book to a predominantly print-linguistic message. While the media attribute of the model emphasizes various media available for composing and delivering the message, print-linguistic messages can be viewed with technology available on most computers and without computer requirements. However, the rhetorical impact of a print document can be affected by technologies associated with them and their delivery in multimodal ways.

For example, a business letter may have a certain impact with letterhead that it does not have without that letterhead. The letterhead adds a visual attribute—and, in some cases, a haptic (or touch) attribute if it is raised—that creates a rhetorical effect. If one receives a message from an attorney's office on letterhead, the message may seem a bit more intimidating than if there was not a letterhead at all. The letterhead seems to add ethos to the message. If that letterhead is raised, it may further add a perception of importance.

This effect extends to the envelope in which the letter or document is contained. An envelope with letterhead, especially raised letterhead, may affect an audience differently than one without letterhead. A large envelope may be perceived as carrying a message that is more important than one contained in a smaller envelope.

A letter that is delivered directly to someone's office by the mail carrier and requires the recipient's signature to verify delivery may, also, create a certain response from the reader/recipient that it would not have had without that activity—the physical presence of the mail carrier and the action of having to sign for it. It seems more official, and, consequently, more important. As such, one is more likely to read it immediately.

Certain things associated with just print media can enhance a message's effect and contribute to multimodal rhetoric. In this chapter I provide a specific example of such rhetoric and effect, using the model presented in this book. The message I describe here is an actual message that I sent to the leadership team—president and several vice presidents—of a major insurance provider after my wife and I experienced considerable frustration resolving some problems coordinating our employer-related insurance benefits. While I have changed the names of people and the organizations involved in the letter that I provide to protect the privacy of those involved, I have left the remaining details and message intact. As I composed the message I had several attributes of neuroscience in mind, particularly mirror neurons and reward neurons and plasticity. I also integrate attributes of ethos, logos, and pathos.

I describe the analysis in a way that is different from the way I presented information in other chapters to account for the different medium and kind of message. I start with the rhetorical situation and provide the message, then the analysis.

Situation

As mentioned above, my wife and I had experienced frustration at the inability to coordinate medical coverage between our respective employer-related benefits. Coordination of benefits occurs when multiple insurers are involved in possible coverage of related members, and it is the act of contacting each insurer to indicate which insurance carrier is the primary insurance and which is secondary for billing purposes. My wife and I had insurance coverage for our family as a full-time employee of our respective employers. My employer offered coverage through one of the particular carriers, and my wife's employer provided coverage through another carrier. While coverage was provided by different companies, the two companies were actually affiliated with each other. In spite of our efforts to coordinate benefits, carriers confused which was the primary and which was the secondary insurance; and we continued to receive bills for care that was covered.

My wife and I had made several phone calls—to both insurance companies and to billing offices—to try to correct the situation; but our efforts seemed always to fail. Our experience is detailed in the letter. A staff member at a billing office shared with my wife an experience she had with her family that was similar to ours. She even provided what she thought was happening to cause the errors. I decided to contact the leadership team of the main insurance carrier for several reasons: I was frustrated at the amount of time it was taking to correct the issue; and because the companies were affiliated with each other, it should not have been that difficult to coordinate benefits between the two companies. Also, recognizing that ours was not unique and the issue may be internal to the companies, I thought that the leadership team needed to be aware of the experiences involving multiple units within its entities.

I searched for e-mail or phone contact information on the company's website but found none. The only contact information I could find was the address of the headquarters. So, I decided to write a letter detailing the situation and problem. In business writing pedagogy parlance, the letter would be considered a "claim letter."

I addressed the letter to the president of the company, and I copied several vice presidents. The audience is the company's leadership team, and the purpose of the message is to address a problem with coordination of benefits. The message, in its entirety, is provided in the next pages. I addressed it directly to the president of the company, because multiple units of the business seemed to be contributing to the problem. Had I ascertained that only one unit was involved, I am sure that I would have addressed only that vice president.

I sent each copy of the message to the recipients in a U.S. Postal Service express mail envelope. It is just a little larger than the size of standard paper, and it is of a heavier stock than standard paper or standard envelopes. I was able not to fold the paper containing the message and enclosures. The pages of the message and the enclosures were paper-clipped together inside the envelope.

Message
1234 Some St
Anywhere, ST 34567
April 11, 20xx

Ronald Smith, Chairman, President and Chief Executive Officer
Medical Insurer Co.
1111 ST
Somewhere

Dear Mr. Cameron:
I am a customer of Medical Insurer through The University's heath care plans, and my wife is a customer of Health Insurer through her employer. I write to express dismay and frustration with recent experiences related to multiple patient accounts and an inability to coordinate benefits between Medical Insurer and Health Insurer, which are part of the same company. My wife and I have done what your customer service personnel have asked us to do in addressing bills from This Hospital and That Hospital; yet, we continue to receive past due notices and bills from these medical providers. The hospital billing staff have acknowledged their frustrations in dealing with customers insured through the two entities, also. So, our case is not unique. I am writing to you in particular, because we perceive an issue with multiple units within your companies

and because **our experience is counter to Medical Insurer's stated service philosophy and values.**

In the past, I have had very good experiences with Medical Insurer as my primary insurer. However, the experiences my wife and I have had in the past year have not met with that same satisfaction. Our case has created frustration for us for the past 7 months. If it is our error, we do not know what to do to correct it; our phone calls have not worked. If it is an internal issue, there is a clear lack of communication between your companies, and the information system(s) involved is/are lacking effective coordination within it or between them. In any case, our experience has been far from Medical Insurer's service philosophy of ....[paraphrasing passages related to carrier's philosophy from their Website ...] (Medical Insurer Website: "Our Values").

I received a third notice of past due payment in January on service rendered over a year ago for .... My wife and I both had coverage through our respective employer (please see the copied member cards; they are this year's cards). In previous months, I received messages indicating reasons for lack of coverage; and these generally involved coordination of benefits issues, not rejection or coding errors. This issue took over x months to resolve as it applied to one of my daughters; my wife and I made several phone calls each week for about a month. I am also in the midst of dealing with a similar situation related to surgery....(see 3rd enclosure). I just received another bill related to it as April began, and a statement related to it from Health Insurer arrived this past week indicating adverse determination due to lack of coordination of benefits (4th enclosure). In most of these cases, as with the 4th enclosure, we were told that the secondary insurer needed to know how much the primary insurer paid out. Again, the two companies are connected; so, I hope you can understand our frustration at this challenge. This should not be difficult to ascertain internally.

My wife and I have contacted the medical provider regarding each of these accounts, and they encouraged us to contact our insurance providers. My wife and I have each contacted both Medical Insurer (MI) and Health Insurer (HI), and each time we were told that they would follow up on the account. I have spoken on different occasions with Someone (HI), Another (HI) and More (MI). They generally take down information from both insurance accounts and say they will follow up. My wife and I have provided EOBs as well. We, then, contact the hospital/medical provider to encourage them to resubmit the claim.

Hospital billing departments know of the issues associated with coordination of benefits between the two entities. Multiple billing personnel have expressed sympathy with our situation. One, at This Hospital's billing department, acknowledged that she has experienced the same problems from other patients who have MI and HI coverage, and it has affected her own family as well. She understands that the MI/HI computer system becomes confused and automatically uses the first name it recognizes alphabetically as the primary insurer. That could explain the problem in our case as well.

If One's conclusion is accurate, the information systems between your companies need to be better developed and coordinated to facilitate better communication and categorization as primary or secondary insurer between the two entities. Again, **this experience and what we are hearing from medical providers' billing offices are contrary to Medical Insurer's service philosophy of** ...[again paraphrasing from Website].... **Because it may affect our financial credit status, forcing us to pay for services that should be paid by the insurer, the experience also challenges your philosophy of** ...[value-related philosophy paraphrased].

On a personal level, I hope you can understand our frustration that the company does not seem able to coordinate with its own entities and the communication challenges we have faced as customers trying to address any errors on our part; it has been anything but accurate and simple. These coordination issues may lead to our accounts going to collection, negatively affecting our personal credit. This does not create peace of mind or trust in your companies to do things right. I am confident that you and your leadership team would fight aggressively to ascertain the cause of such an issue if it affected you and them as it has us. On a professional level, I will use this to teach business students how to address such communication issues; and I hope you will use it to help improve communication at your companies.

I teach professional writing courses at The University, and I coordinate the business writing course required of all business majors at TU. We often use case studies to facilitate analyses and reports simulating 'real world' scenarios, as I am sure you and your leadership team recall from your and their educational experiences. This is an excellent example of a series of communication-related problems affecting a business internally and externally.

I recall in my own business education experience a professor who provided us with information about how a specific company responded to a scenario that we had just worked on as a case study. It was fascinating to compare how we handled the situation with how the company actually handled it and the result. I will share your response with our students.

Finally, as a study in leadership, this case can be used to demonstrate how closely committed a leadership team is to its company's philosophies and values. I graduated from the Leadership Institute, The University's leadership development program, in 20xx. We often discussed links between a company's values and users'/customers' experiences. When the user's/customer's experience does not match the company's values/philosophy, there is a problem.

Your company strives to create peace of mind for customers. That has not been our experience in the past several months, and it sounds like others are having similar experiences with your companies.

Thank you for considering our experience and looking into remedies for it. I look forward to your response.

Sincerely,
Dirk Remley

Enclosures (4)
xc:
Mr. X, Executive Vice President and Chief Communications Officer
Ms. Y, Executive Vice President and Chief Information Officer
Ms. Z Larkins, Executive Vice President and Chief Marketing Officer
Ms. T, Executive Vice President and Chief Customer Experience Officer

Analysis

I introduce the topic and purpose in the opening paragraph—standard in any business writing setting. I also make an immediate connection to the company's values and philosophy; these will appeal to the audience quickly. Leadership is always concerned about how the company is meeting its corporate mission, philosophy, and values. I am aware that in some executive-level settings, presentations need to begin with an explicit reference to the topic's positioning within the company's mission and philosophies; that is how important those elements are to a company's leadership. This "move" combines a pathetic and logical appeal that is based on neural plasticity associated with leadership development.

In the second paragraph, I provide some "good feeling" message (previous experiences); but I call attention to the specific issue, again, referring explicitly to the company values and philosophy. I even cite the company website, showing that I have researched the company. This re-enforces the plasticity element of leadership's concern for such issues as well as establishes my own ethos—I know about the company's values.

I describe our experience in paragraphs three through five, alluding to the fact that hospital billing departments have observed a problem. This is, also, a logical appeal drawing on reward neurons of the audience; if others are noting a problem, this is bad for the company's reputation. Further, the readers can check on it by asking those people directly. The leadership team will want to correct the problem quickly, before there is a public relations problem.

In paragraph six, I allude to the billing department staffer's speculation about a cause, linking it to our experience as well as linking it to the company's values and philosophy. Again, the statement about the billing staffer's observations contributes to my own ethos as a credible source of information; they can check on it. Connecting our experience to the company's values involves logical and pathetic appeals based on reward neuron dynamics and plasticity of leadership's values. In leadership's experience, they have emphasized these principles internally; they are used to expressing action relative to those values and philosophies. Further, an outsider is making a direct appeal to those values, calling attention to how the experience does not match what the values express.

Paragraphs seven through ten are where I actively and explicitly integrate mirror neurons—facilitating connections between me and the audience. Basically, I refer to my own experiences in a leadership position, my business education (which they have also experienced; they all hold the MBA degree, I learned from researching their background on the company website), and my experience in a leadership training program, which most of them have experienced. I am able to help them understand that I am not dramatically different from them with respect to our leadership backgrounds. While I am not just like them in terms of leading a large company, my intention is to show that I am able to appreciate some of the elements affecting leaders better than many others may be able to do. I appeal to them on a personal level as well as professional; leaders are human and have a personal life. They would understand the frustration such errors can cause on a personal level. This is mostly a pathetic appeal, drawing on ethos—mine and theirs—and logos; mine are logical concerns based on the evidence presented; the documentation showing delays and potential impact on credit rating.

In paragraph ten I try to integrate an appeal to reward neurons, but I do not know how the readers would respond to it. By mentioning that I will share their response with my students, I hope that they perceive potential reward by acting on the situation and corresponding a certain way, making them look favorable. As I note, they likely experienced that discussion in their MBA programs—hearing about how a company responded to a specific case as part of a case study follow-up. If the company responded well, the students probably felt it made the company look good. That reinforces my ethos (not only am I in a leadership positon; I can share this case with many students of business—including the response of this leadership team), plays on pathos (they will feel better if the company is perceived favorably), and integrates potential reward (they and the company look good in light of a favorable response).

In terms of media, again, I sent this as a letter; so, one would perceive lack of multimodal effect. However, there is a multimodal effect related to spatial and visual appearance. I did not include university letterhead, because it was not university-related. However, I use bold in a few paragraphs, and I sent copies of it in 9"x12" express mail envelopes to their offices. The bold typeface integrates a visual attribute beyond "normal" typeface. So, it would get their attention and emphasize particular information. Also, I hoped the envelopes would stand out from other mail they may have received, taking up a bit more space than standard letter envelopes. The "express mail" design on the envelope, further, gave it a more important look than a regular envelope—standard or 9"x12" sized.

Further, I included my business card, documenting my position. This is an ethical appeal that draws on plasticity associated with "official" business practices, and eliciting mirror neurons. Business people share business cards as part of a formal introduction. I am mirroring a standard practice they are used to experiencing. My business card includes the university logo as well as my title and contact information. Like that letterhead, the logo bears a given official message itself. The card, also, reinforces my own ethos, caring information about my personal website to document my background, in case one of the recipients wants to look into that.

There is an element of temporal synchronicity and intermodal redundancy, too. The reader/recipient feels the envelope as they open it to access the letter; it feels large, which may create the perception of importance. It certainly gets their attention. So, the size of the envelope has a visual and touch (haptic)-related effect.

The letter may seem more important, too, coming from a large envelope that included the visual stimuli associated with the words "Express delivery" and other colorful text on the envelope's design. So, the letter is accessed just after the visual and haptic experiences associated with the envelope's size, eliciting the perception of importance. Finally, the contents of the envelope involved no fewer than seven pages and a business card; it feels thick. I did not use the larger envelope just to create a rhetorical effect; it would have been impractical to try to fold all of the pages involved into a standard letter mailing envelope. The thickness of the message packet may also create the perception of importance relative to the visual and haptic attributes associated with size.

Attention-Modal Filtering is accomplished by the limited use of modes—visual and touch, and the required progression from envelope to pulling out the contents to reading the letter and enclosures. The reader is not overwhelmed by the experience because they are used to opening mail, including large mail envelopes in their previous experiences. I have also appealed to their previous experiences as described above relative to plasticity-related attributes.

Result

I received a phone call from someone who introduced herself as the president's assistant about a week after sending the message. She acknowledged that the leadership team had received the letter and had talked about it at some length. The president gave it to her and asked her to look into the situation. She had reviewed our phone calls and other documentation (when they say, "This call may be recorded for quality-control purposes...." believe it; she had been reviewing those recordings, which documented our calls to the company).

Over the course of several weeks, as she reviewed files and made phone calls, the situation was corrected. Eventually, I received a letter from one of the VPs, in which she indicated new steps the company was taking to assure such a situation did not happen again generally. She also indicated the action they had taken with the assistant to work with us closely to address any and all bills that were erroneously sent to us.

Even as we received new bills for services other than those mentioned in the letter, we maintained contact with the assistant to address any bill we perceived had not been properly handled, and she responded to each situation directly. The president's assistant is now our direct contact within the company.

Conclusion

What seems to be an entirely "print" business document/message can be considered to be multimodal, depending on certain attributes of the format of the message as well as the media associated with delivery. The rhetorical effectiveness of these messages can be affected by decisions regarding such format and delivery.

12 Conclusion

Having illustrated several examples of the application of neuroscientific analysis to a review of multimodal persuasive rhetoric, I conclude with this chapter in which I identify implications for integrating this kind of analysis into education and business. I have alluded to certain kinds of multimodal persuasive rhetoric with each chapter, but I make connections between the concepts described earlier and application explicit here. I do that because scholarship recognizes the value of making information explicit in instructional capacities. This is the first implication of implementing these concepts into instructions and training—explicit instruction of neuroscientific concepts in pedagogy and training of multimodal persuasive messages.

Explicit Versus Implicit Instruction

Columb (2010) acknowledges that in writing courses explicit teaching is "intended to bring about identifiable effects on qualities, features or other aspects of writing" (slide 6). He summarizes arguments against explicit teaching in writing courses as indicating that writing does not involve conscious processes and, therefore, writing is learned through subconscious processes (slide 6). However, he challenges this by explaining that parts of writing are consciously understood, including planning, drafting, and revising (slide 7). He also acknowledges that "nonconscious processes can be influenced by consciously created dispositions"; that is, if one is aware that a particular rhetorical strategy can work in a given situation, he or she will consciously apply it (slide 8).

Several studies find differences between explicit instruction, implicit instruction, and learning (see, for example, Ziemer-Andrews, 2007; Morrison, Bachman, and McDonald-Conner, 2005; and Leblanc and Lally, 1998). They find that students learn complex topics better when they receive explicit instruction in that topic, while there seems to be little statistically significant difference in learning simple topics relative to either approach.

For example, I detailed an example of connections between neuroscience and narrative in Chapter 5. While narrative is a popular genre for helping students develop as writers, Rentz (1992) observes that it is difficult to distinguish narrative from many other forms of discourse because various elements of narrative occur in other genres as well. In each of the messages I provided there was some kind of narrative involved. In most cases here it was part of an effort to elicit mirror neurons toward helping the audience perceive a shared experience or emotion with the speaker.

Rentz states, "we understand much, if not all, of our experience in narrative form, so that even those things we write that do not take the shape of narrative have been distilled from our original narrative-like understanding of what we are writing about" (p. 299). While narrative itself is not persuasive in nature, it can be used within persuasive messages. Rentz distinguishes narrative from argument by characterizing narrative as concerned with the particular instead of with generalizations, holistic rather than a composite of different parts, and providing a quality of reflection (p. 297). Narrative can be used simply to report information; however, it can also function within persuasion, as illustrated with the examples in Chapter 5.

The prevalence of narrative in examples of professional writing found in textbooks echoes its uses in practice. Though personal narratives engage students in writing about a topic with which they are intimately familiar, professional narratives tend to integrate professional discourses and an understanding of how professionals in a given field think about a phenomenon. However, the law firm advertising example I used above shows an effort to address a general public audience. Including explicit instruction in narrative and neural dynamics associated with it in business writing pedagogy and in textbooks will help students refine those skills and understand how they are used in the workplace.

In technical writing and business writing pedagogy, students learn various forms of professional writing—correspondence, report writing, proposals, resumes, and manuals—that integrate forms of narrative. Also, as they review professionals' writing, students come to learn discipline-specific discourse and practice it as well in their own writing on assignments and exercises. In the next section, I offer suggestions to help textbook authors and instructors integrate explicit instruction in it. I also suggest further research regarding the impact that such instruction may have on learning and practicing narrative skills.

Suggestions for Explicit Instruction of Narrative and Neurorhetoric of It

Students need the opportunity to hone skills associated with developing effective narratives in coursework. Including explicit instruction in narrative, including neural contents associated with it, in technical writing and business writing pedagogy and in textbooks used in these classes will help students refine those skills and understand how to use them in the workplace.

Authors of business writing and technical writing textbooks can accomplish this explicit inclusion of narrative by:

1   Integrating explicit references to narrative and neural responses in examples of persuasive multimodal messages, and
2   Integrating references to attributes of narratives in sections explaining style components and distinguishing narratives from more formal, objective forms of reporting information, and
3   Showing examples of narrative-style persuasive messages and discussing rhetorical and neural attributes, much as I have done in this book.

Teachers can encourage students to think about rhetorical and neural attributes of their own persuasive messages within grading rubrics and reflection. A grading rubric for a multimodal persuasive assignment, for example, might include a category specifically listing possible neural responses associated with mirror neurons and reward neurons.

Table 12.1 is an example rubric that could be used for assessing both multimodal instructional material and multimodal persuasive material. It lists seven different categories based on the model, totaling 21 points. It also offers a holistic interpretation of the assessment.

As stated before, cognition relative to a persuasive message would be equivalent to perception. So, in an instructional message, cognition pertains to how well the audience would understand the new concept/task and be able to learn the concept/task; in a persuasive message the cognition row would characterize how well the product affects perception generally toward the desired perception and related action.

Also, many faculty encourage students to reflect on their composing process, especially within multimodal assignments. Such reflections can include description of how the student perceives their message stimulates certain neurons in addition to integrating the other rhetorical attributes of the model provided in this book that influence the perceived effectiveness of the message. Such a narrative could be used to provide the student's perception of the product's effectiveness relative to the model and rubric. That narrative may help the teacher/trainer assess the product as well.

Business consultants and trainers can use these ideas as well in their training in corporate settings. For example, one activity could encourage attendees to consider specific rhetorical principles and neural responses to a given message as they develop a marketing tool for a given product or service their company offers.

Table 12.1 Sample Rubric

	Very Effective (3 points)	Moderately Effective (2 points)	Ineffective (1 point)
Medium/media used [considering affordances/constraints of the tool used to deliver the message; how effective is that tool/those tools for the message and audience?]			
Narrative [how well does the message convey the desired action and consider the audience's perspective?]			
Visual Dominance [Is a visualization of the object/subject provided or easy to make from the information? Is an image of the speaker/presenter provided; if so, what impression does it make?]			
Modal-Attention Filtering [How effectively do modes help to affect attention? How many modes are used—enough/too much/not enough—and do they help to focus attention?]			
Temporal Synchronicity [how effectively are the modes timed to allow appropriate filtering of information and cognition?]			

Intermodal Redundancy [how effectively do the modes re-enforce each other or provide information to enhance the message in different ways?]

Prior Experience: Mirror Neurons [how effectively does the creator use attributes of the audience's prior experiences to elicit mirroring dynamics: e.g.: values about status/groups of people/representations of dress?]

Prior Experience: Reward Neurons [how effectively does the creator use attributes of the audience's prior experiences that would elicit reward neurons: e.g.; values/motivations/goals]

Cognition [holistic interpretation: how effectively does the product help the audience understand what the message is and what the audience should do?]

Score above 18:
If most criteria are assessed as very effective, it suggests that the product is very good at facilitating cognition of the desired action and very persuasive.

Score between 15 and 18:
If most criteria are assessed as moderately effective, it suggests that some items could be improved to make it a better product. The audience may not understand the desired action or not be as moved to act as desired as it otherwise could be if information were presented differently.

Score below 15:
If most criteria are assessed as ineffective, it suggests that several items need to be improved upon. The audience is not likely to be moved toward action because the product does not engage the audience well or facilitate understanding of the desired action well.

Dress Codes

Professionals tend to have a dress code to which they conform for work settings, whether that dress code is explicitly announced by a company or the professional implicitly assigns one to him or herself, depending on their profession. Such a dress code may be characterized as "business formal" or "business casual;" in some companies, there may even be a "dress down Friday" when employees can wear generally casual dress—polo shirt and jeans, for example. I detailed examples of the application of dress code as part of multimodal rhetoric in certain persuasive messages in Chapter 6. It is a good idea to encourage students and professionals to consider a dress code as they prepare to give presentations or attend certain meetings.

This practice is typical in almost any educational setting requiring an oral presentation; a class may have a required dress code to adhere to as part of the presentations; each presenter must dress professionally, and this will be part of the grade for their presentation. Teachers who integrate presentation into their courses can encourage students to research dress codes within their major area of study. What kind of dress is expected of marketing managers, for example? What kind of dress is a public relations professional expected to have when meeting clients? Engage students with expectations of professionals within their field through Internet research or interviews with such professionals.

Further, instructors can integrate a reflective exercise in the course in which students explicitly connect their dress for a particular presentation to the expectations of the audience and rhetoric associated with it. In Chapter 6 I mentioned the example of the graduating student who wore a polo shirt and sporty pants to an interview, violating the interviewer's expectations of professionalism. If one wears an informal outfit when giving a presentation to a certain group of people that expects more professional dress, how does that impact the general rhetoric of the presentation's message?

Teachers and trainers alike can show video of people in different dress making presentations and have students/trainees consider for what audiences each dress is best suited for the particular presentation. Much as politicians dress down when making "folksy" campaign visits to a local restaurant show their connection with "common folk," certain audiences may find a dressed down look more appealing for a given persuasive message than a more formal look.

Possible Cases to Use Within Instruction and Training

Consider scenarios you encounter with some regularity: children on fundraising efforts for a local school district or social organization (baked goods fundraisers or Girl Scout cookies, for example); receiving a promotional mailer/flier about a new product or sale at a local store;

automotive vehicle commercials. These can be used as scenarios/cases for analysis and development.

Why do I never feel compelled to purchase a magazine subscription from the high schooler trying to raise money for his or her school district while also trying to earn enough credit to go to Myrtle Beach for a week for free? Generally, how does such a person tend to approach the situation; what is their typical "pitch" and what is their tone of voice as they present it (hint: it is usually focused on "...and if I sell x subscriptions I can go to Myrtle Beach for free.")? When do they present the list of magazines from which to choose and what does that list look like? How do they usually dress when they are on this mission? An activity could be to analyze this encounter using the model and, then, develop a better way for the high schooler to approach the situation using the model again.

One could ask students or trainees to evaluate a particular flier or print advertisement and then have the student/trainee develop a better product using the same medium/media. For example, what considerations may have affected the design of the provided product (e.g.: cost for color printing or particular demographic/psychographic attributes of targeted market)? A company may have used a social medium for a particular advertisement to reach a 20–35 demographic, recognizing that many people in that demographic use that tool; how could the advertisement have been improved within that same medium?

Further Research Implications

Narrative

Empirical study of narrative's treatment in business writing and technical writing and neural dynamics of it therein could include both analyses of texts and audience responses. I would encourage a survey of responses to various persuasive messages on a national level. Local surveys of professionals, for example, would likely attest to the geographic demographic attitudes, which could be observed statistically, identifying patterns in neural plasticity in local regions. A national survey would provide an aggregate of these observations toward identifying general responses/perceptions of such messages.

Interdisciplinary research is a challenge at many institutions; however, I encourage writing and rhetoric faculty to engage in research with neurobiologists or cognitive psychologists who may have access to fMRI machines or EEG technologies. Such research could identify more specific neural responses associated with various kinds of messages and demographic as well as psychographic attributes of the viewer. Some marketing companies do this for companies; however, scholarship that reports on such experimentation would make the information more public and useful in instruction.

Dress Code

Some scholarship on the rhetoric of dress already exists, but much of it is within communication studies research. Consequently, it is possible to look into the connections between dress and persuasion further through interdisciplinary research. Again, though fMRI scans, researchers can present videos of people in various dress making persuasive pitches and ask them to consider which were more persuasive.

Composition instructors use narrative in general writing classes to help students practice basic writing skills by engaging them in writing about something they know and understand most—their own experiences. Many institutions include multimodal composing within composition coursework to expose students to various composing technologies and give them practice using those tools. Pedagogy beyond the composition level tends to undervalue explicit treatment of narrative in favor of implicit instruction, showing forms of narrative in examples of reports and other messages. However, explicit instruction in narrative as a rhetorical tool that includes discussion of neural dynamics associated with particular messages could enhance learning how to apply it in professional settings.

Blyler and Perkins (1999a and 1999b) as well as Rentz (1992) assert that narrative acts as a rhetorical tool for use in business writing and technical writing settings, and Blyler (1995) and Jameson (2004) acknowledge the value of narrative as a tool to help students understand discourse in professional settings and as a tool for ethnographic study. Professionals use narrative in their communications, and this use can vary from print-linguistic to multimodal. So, instruction in persuasive rhetoric should include discussion of neural dynamics of multimodal messages.

Technological Limitations of Research Tools and Options

As I indicated in *HTB* (2015), research can examine different physical activity as technology advances. Neurobiological research before 2000 emphasized use of EEG technology to collect data, but fMRI technology from which the hemo-neural hypothesis grew helps us understand that various systems in the brain are at work in facilitating cognitive processes as well. However, MRI technologies are still loud, which can affect any aural dynamics associated with multimodal analysis, perception, and even cognition. Until MRI equipment can reduce the noise level to minimally impact sensory attributes that contribute to perception and cognition, it is challenging to account for the noise in an analysis of the impact multimodal materials have on cognition.

While fMRI is able to identify a variety of patterns of neural activity, it may be difficult to account for and address in research the noise and any claustrophobic effects of using it for this research. A more viable approach may be Magnetoencephalography (or MEG) which combines attributes of EEG and fMRI.

MRI machines are very loud and require immersion of the entire head and neck into them. Immersion would limit the ability for one to view any multimodal product, and the noise associated with the machine would practically render any audio associated with a multimodal product ineffective. MEG enables one to view multimodal products without being immersed completely. However, MEG also is not as fast as fMRI and it measures different regions of the brain. So, data between the two tools may not agree with each other (Cohen and Halgren, 2004).

As with any research tool, there are limitations associated with technologies available to measure neural activity. However, research must negotiate with these tools toward facilitating the best research possible.

Pharmacology

The discussion I presented in this book can contribute to pharmacological developments such as developing drugs that treat neurological disorders that affect cognition. Medications that address disorders or conditions such as Attention-Deficit Hyper-Activity Disorder (ADHD) focus on attributes of attention associated with cognition and are applied mostly in instructional settings. Through the same research methods, studies that include analysis of brain activity and integrate the administration of medical drugs can help to ascertain which medications can most effectively treat cognitive problems and help improve cognition in various populations. Such studies may include understanding how medications affect perception and persuasion.

Studies associated with the use of certain medications toward improving cognition or test performance tend to link the use of medications used for treating ADHD with better performance. ADHD has been linked to decreased dopamine levels (see, for example, Volkow et al., 2007). However, it is generally understood that ADHD medications such as Adderall and Ritalin work by increasing the number of neurotransmitters and prolonging their life in synapses. Neurotransmitters, like dopamine neurons, can be created out of amino acids, available from common diets. Categorized as amphetamines, they simply help one to pay attention by stimulating the cells that carry information across neural pathways. A problem with such medications, though, is that they are highly addictive and can lead to damage to neurons as well as other physical problems. If paying attention is the biggest hurdle to overcome, and the patient/subject would otherwise be able to understand a given concept or set of instructions, then such a medication can work well. However, cognition involves more than just paying attention.

Studies of those who have disorders such as Autism can help physicians and teachers understand how people with such conditions process information so they can make informed decisions and avoid confusion about persuasive messages. People with such disorders are part of the voting population and consume products and services. Consequently, interdisciplinary study linking multimodal rhetoric scholarship and neuro-scientific scholarship can contribute to development of new medications and treatments or more effective messages. Biochemistry programs may team with technical communication or multimodal rhetoric programs to develop new curricula that encourage interdisciplinary study and work that contribute to such new treatments and medications.

As certain subjects with neural disorders are studied, the research can include administration of medications that affect neural activity, and fMRI and EEG studies can show how the medication is affecting processes toward cognition.

Closing

As I indicated in Chapter 1, the cognitive experience includes biological as well as social dynamics. Cognitive science and the field of rhetoric, generally, recognize these attributes of cognition—social and biological attributes related to facilitating an understanding of our world. Disciplinary boundaries have compromised the discussion of these cognitive neuroscience dynamics. I have attempted to continue to cross these boundaries in this book with this model. With a model that integrates social and neurobiological attributes of rhetoric to describe the ways our brain processes multimodal information toward cognition, I encourage further studies that combine these diverse perspectives.

Rhetoric considers how an audience reacts relative to the way information is presented. One designs a message to facilitate a certain response from an audience. As Aristotle (translated 1991) and Perelman and Olbrechts-Tyteca (1969) acknowledged, the way a message is conveyed must consider the audience's disposition in order to accomplish its purpose, and this disposition includes one's social disposition or biological/physical disposition. Indeed, Aristotle notes that this likely involves an audience that may have "limited intellectual scope and limited capacity to follow an extended chain of reasoning" (p. 76). If the audience's cognitive capacities are not considered in developing the message, the meaning of the message will be lost. This model attempts to take into consideration both biological and social dimensions of cognition.

Neural process studies help to explain some of the biological attributes connected to findings of multimodal scholarship; that is, they help us understand *why*, from a biological perspective, certain multimodal products facilitate a better understanding of information than other multimodal products, and they also affect perception of reality.

The model I presented in Chapter 3 integrates what I consider to be the five attributes involved in cognition and which are affected by biological and social dynamics. The sixth attribute—medium—frames how one can design a message. This model is shown again in Figure 12.1.

As mentioned in previous chapters, the fields of rhetoric and neurobiology tend to examine multimodal and multisensory experiences differently, using different tools especially. Rhetoric studies tend to focus attention on composition and observed behaviors or surveys of audience perception of content; neurobiological studies focus on particular neuron behaviors inside the brain based on biomedical technologies. However, these neurobiological studies involve analysis of such activity relative to certain stimuli. Rhetoric can contribute to such studies, and the field of rhetoric can benefit from integrated studies likewise. Interdisciplinary research, facilitated by a model that engages the scholarship of multiple disciplines, can help with the development of better instructional designs and tools.

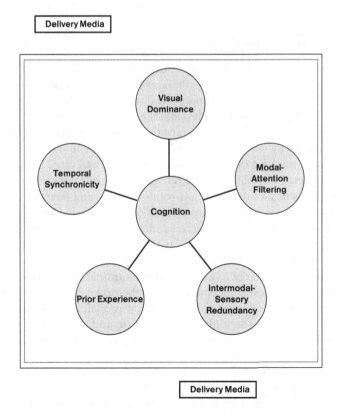

Figure 12.1 Model.

In each chapter of this book, in addition to citing specific studies, I alluded to varying degrees to persuasive messages relatively common in our daily lives. Given how often we encounter multimodal information that our brain tries to process toward cognition, it is troubling to know that comprehensive study of such dynamics is hindered by the disciplinary divisions I have mentioned. The model I presented in this book is a way to synthesis scholarship in the different fields productively.

Examples of potential studies include ascertaining how the brain processes certain modal combinations; rhetoric scholars can design these combinations and use common approaches in social science research to contribute data to joint studies. Studies that include both biomedical technologies as well as social science research methods such as surveys and interviews with participants as well as observation and quasi-experimental designs can triangulate each other.

There are grants available through the National Institute for Humanities as well as foundations commonly associated with biomedical science research such as the National Science Foundation. Joint research can facilitate triangulation of information, leading to development of effective persuasive materials that consider a population's disposition.

Directions for Future Growth

Earlier in this chapter, I identified ways that interdisciplinary research that integrated the model could enhance education and training as well as facilitate developments in pharmaceutical treatments. Here I suggest paths that scholarship may take to develop the model proposed in this book more fully. I mentioned in the Preface that the model is an early effort at finding a means by which interdisciplinary research can occur. I also indicated that the model is descriptive. It describes various attributes of cognition of any new information, but I recognize that it is not comprehensive.

Because it is in its infancy, it has room to grow and develop. I encourage scholars to pursue development of it likewise, crossing their own disciplinary boundaries by conducting research with scholars in other disciplines or applying it to their own research as I have, toward adding attributes to this model so it may represent a more comprehensive model of cognition.

Some questions emerge to guide further examination and development of the model. I ask researchers to consider their own disciplinary theories and how they may be integrated into the new model. I have characterized connections between the multimodal rhetoric and neurobiology of cognition, and I open the door to other consideration with these questions:

1　What principles of the model presented here seem similar to attributes of theories of cognition and persuasion in other field(s)?

2　Can such attributes be merged with the particular principles of the model to explain more fully that particular principle's relationship to cognition of new information?

3 Does a new nomenclature need to be developed, or can existing terms from different fields be used and synthesized, as the term "multimodal" was able to be synthesized between "multimodal rhetoric" and "multimodal integration," to characterize principles of multimodality here?

4 What attributes of cognition are not identified yet within the model? Does a new principle need to be added, or can one be developed further? That is, do some principles require sub-principles? The principles I provided carry over from my discussion of the model relative to instructional materials; do they need to be changed at all given a different rhetorical purpose?

Related to Question 1, I would consider how the model may apply to Toulmin's (2003) model of argument. Are the two mutually exclusive or can principals from both be integrated? I would respond that they can be integrated into a single analysis. I do not include a chapter or application related to that in this book; however, it is something that one could pursue further; how prior experience, for example, affects "backing" within an argument, or how certain data are valued or not because of how that data may be perceived relative to how it is presented or due to one's experiences. How do factors associated with this model affect cognition and the structure of an argument within Toulmin's model?

Particularly related to Question 4, can the principle of prior experience adequately address cultural attributes of language and cognition, or does a new principle need to be added to the model to address such attributes?

The kinds of interdisciplinary research that I have suggested can address these questions. Ultimately, the improvements made to persuasive messages and one's understanding of reality are what matter most, but an integrated model will enable researchers to consider the many attributes of cognition better toward developing those materials and improving comprehension.

References

Allman, B., Keniston, L., & Meredith, M. A. (2009). Not just for multimodal neurons anymore: The contribution of unimodal neurons to cortical multi-sensory processing. *Brain Topography, 21*, 157–167.

Allman, B. & Meredith, A. M. (2007). Multisensory processing in 'unimodal' neurons: Cross-modal subthreshold auditory effects in cat extrastriate visual cortex. *Journal of Neurophysiology, 98*, 545–549.

Arias-Carrion, O. & Poppel, E. (2007). Dopamine, learning, and reward-seeking behavior. *Acta neurobiologiae experimentalis. 67*(4), 481–488.

Aristotle. (1991). *The art of rhetoric* (H. C. Lawson-Tancred, Trans). London: Penguin.

Arnheim, R. (1969). *Visual thinking*. Berkeley: University of California Press.

Azar, B. (2010). More powerful persuasion. *Monitor on Psychology, 41*, pp. 36–38. Retrieved from http://www.scn.ucla.edu/pdf/Persuasion-Monitor-2010.pdf.

Baddeley, A. D. (1986). *Working memory*. Oxford: Oxford University Press.

Ball, C. (2006). Designerly ≠ readerly: Re-assessing multimodal and new media rubrics for use in writing studies. *Convergence: The International Journal of Research into New Media Technologies, 12*, 393–412.

Beemer, C., Bowles, S., & Shaver, L. (2005). At your service: Teaching rhetoric in a business school writing center. *Praxis: A Writing Center Journal, 3.1*.

Berlucchi, G. & Buchtel, H. A. (2009). Neuronal plasticity: Historical roots and evolution of meaning. *Experimental Brain Research, 192*(3), 307–319.

Bernstein, L. E., Auer, E. T. Jr., & Moore, J. K. (2004). Audiovisual speech binding: Convergence or association? In Calvert, G., Spence, C. & Stein, B. E. (eds.). *The handbook of multisensory processes* (pp. 203–223). Cambridge: MIT Press.

Bethge, M., Rotermund, D., & Pawelzik, K. (2003). Optimal neural rate coding leads to multimodal firing rate distributions. *Computational Neural Systems, 14*, 303–319.

Bichot N. P. & Desimone, R. (2006). Finding a face in the crowd: parallel and serial neural mechanisms of visual selection. *Programming Brain Res* 155: 147–156. In Moore, C. I. & Cao, R. (2008). The Hemo-Neural Hypothesis: On the role of blood flow in information processing. *Journal of Neurophysiology, 99*, 2035–2047.

Bizley, J. K. & King, A. J. (2012). What can multisensory processing tell us about the functional organization of auditory cortex? In Murray, M. M. & Wallace, M. T. (eds.). *The neural bases of multisensory processes* (pp. 31–48). Boca Raton: CRC Press.

Blyler, N. R. (1995). Pedagogy and social action: A role for narrative in professional communication. *Journal of Business and Technical Communication, 9*, 289–320.

Blyler, N. R. (1996). Narrative and research in professional communication. *Journal of Business and Technical Communication, 10*, 330–351.

Blyler, N. R. & Perkins, J. (1999a). Guest editors' introduction: Culture and the power of narrative. *Journal of Business and Technical Communication, 13*, 245–248.

Blyler, N. R. & Perkins, J. (eds.) (1999b). *Narrative and professional communication.* New York: Ablex Publishing Co.

Boudreau, C., Coulson, S., & McCubbins, M. D. (2011). Pathways to persuasion: How neuroscience can inform the study and practice of law. pp. 395–406. In Freeman, M. (ed.) (2011). *Law and neuroscience: Current legal issues 2010.* (Volume 13). New York: Oxford UP.

Bouwman, H., van den Hoof, B., van de Wijngaert, L., & Dijk, J. (2005). *Information and communication technology in organizations: Adaptation, implementation, use and effects.* London: Sage.

Bremner, A. J. & Spence, C. (2008). Unimodal experience constrains while multisensory experiences enrich cognitive construction. *Behavioral and Brain Sciences, 31*, 335–336.

Brooks, R. A. & Stein, L. A. (1994). Building brains for bodies. *Autonomous Robots, 1*, 7–25.

Calvert, G., Spence, C., & Stein, B. (eds.) (2004). *The handbook of multisensory processes.* Cambridge: MIT Press.

Campos, J. L. & Bulthoff, H. H. (2012). Multimodal integration during self-motion in virtual reality. In Murray, M. & Wallace, M. (eds.). *The neural bases of multisensory processes* (pp. 603–628). Boca Raton; CRC Press.

Cao, R. (2011). The hemo-neural hypothesis: effects of vasodilation on astrocytes in mammalian neocortex. Thesis. MIT.

Capraro, L. (2011). The juridicial role of emotions in decisional process of popular juries. In Freeman, M. (editor). *Law and neuroscience: Current legal issues* 2010. (Volume 13). pp. 407–417. New York: Oxford UP.

Cartwright, S. (2014). How and why businesses make use of Scent Marketing to boost sales. Website Designs. https://website-designs.com/online-marketing/scent-marketing/scent-marketing-to-boost-sales/ December 23, 2014.

Center for Disease Control. (2015). Marlene. Retrieved from www.plowsharegroup.com/cdctips.

www.city-data.com/city/a.

www.city-data.com/city/b.

Clemo, H. R., Keniston, L. P., & Meredith, M. A. (2012). Structural basis of multisensory processing: Convergence. In Murray, M. & Wallace, M. (eds.). *The neural bases of multisensory processes* (pp. 3–14). Boca Raton; CRC Press.

Cohen, D. & Halgren, E. (2004). "Magnetoencephalography." In Adelman, G. & Smith, B. (eds.). *Encyclopedia of Neuroscience*, Elsevier, 1st, 2nd, and 3rd (2004) editions.

Colavita, F. B. (1974). Human sensory dominance. *Perception & Psychophysics, 16*, 409–412.

Colorado Oil and Gas Association. (2015). Hickenlooper ad. Retrieved from http://www.coga.org/audio/Gov_Hickenlooper_HF_Rule_30sec.mp3 (audio file).

Columb, Greg. (2010). Framework for a theory of explicit teaching. Retrieved from: http://faculty.virginia.edu/schoolhouse/CCCC2010/Colomb ExplicitTeaching.pdf.

Denning, S. (2005). *The Leader's Guide to Story-Telling: Mastering the Art of Business Narrative*. New York: John Wiley and Sons, Inc.

Donahue, S. E., Woldorff, M. G., & Mitroff, S. R. (2010). Video game players show more precise multisensory temporal processing abilities. *Attention, Perception and Psychophysics, 72*, 1120–1129.

Dooley, R. (2012). Brainfluence: 100 ways to persuade and convince consumers within neuromarketing. Hoboken, John Wiley and Sons.

Elmer, M. (2004). Multisensory integration: How visual experience shapes spatial perception. *Current Biology, 14*, R115–R117.

Energy From Shale. (2015a). TV: Dillon, Colorado. Retrieved from https://www.youtube.com/watch?v=3SdR2SVUOdY (video file).

Energy From Shale, (2015b). TV: Safe for Our Land: Oil and Natural Gas in Colorado. Retrieved from https://www.youtube.com/watch?v=8sbhMdPx_NA (video file).

Fleming, D. (2001). Narrative leadership: using the power of stories. Originally appeared in *Strategy & Leadership 29*. 4. http://www.makingstories.net/narrative_leadership_by_David_Fleming.pdf.

Freeman, M. (ed.) (2011). *Law and Neuroscience: Current Legal Issues* 2010. (Volume 13). New York: Oxford UP.

Friedman, Domiano, & Smith. (2015). Jeff Friedman's Story. Retrieved from https://www.fdslaw.com/about-us/jeffs-story.php.

Gallese, V., Eagle, M. N., & Migone, P. (2007). Intentional attunement: Mirror neurons and the neural underpinnings of interpersonal relations. *Journal of the American Psychoanalytic Association, 55*, 131–176.

Gass, R. H. & Seiter, J. S. (2014). *Persuasion: Social influence and compliance gaining*. Abingdon: Routledge.

Gee, J. P. (2003). *What video games have to teach us about learning and literacy*. New York: Palgrave McMillan.

Gopnic, A., Meltzoff, A., & Kuhl, P. (1999). *The scientist in the crib: What early learning tells us about the mind*. New York: HarperCollins Publishers.

Gorn, G. J., Chattopahyay, A., Sengupta, J., & Tripathi, S. (2004). Waiting for the Web: how screen color affects time. *Journal of Marketing Research, 41*, 215–225.

Gross C. G. (1998). *Brain vision memory: Tales in the history of neuroscience*. Cambridge: MIT Press.

Gruber, D. R. (2012). Neurorhetoric and the Dynamism of the Neurosciences: Mapping Translations of Mirror Neurons Across the Disciplines. Unpublished dissertation. North Carolina State University.

Help Me Colorado (2014a). The Oligarch. Retrieved from https://www.youtube.com/watch?v=SfNzW9YY8QE. (video file).

Help Me Colorado (2014b). Make it rain and help me stay rich Colorado. Retrieved from https://www.youtube.com/watch?v=SfNzW9YY8QE (video file).

Help Me Colorado (2014c). I need Chauffeurs: Help me Stay Rich Colorado. Retrieved from https://www.youtube.com/watch?v=7Igd3xN3FuM (video file).

Herrington, A., Hodgson, K., & Moran, C. (2009). Technology, change and assessment: What we have learned. In A. Herrington, K. Hodgson, and C. Moran (eds.). *Teaching the new writing: Technology, change and assessment in the 21st Century classroom* (pp. 198–208). New York: Teachers College Press.

Hewett, B. L., Remley, D., Zemliansky, P., & Dipardo, A. (2010). Frameworks for talking about collaborative writing. In *Virtual collaborative writing in the workplace: Technologies and processes.* (pp. 28–51). Hewett, B.L. and Robidoux, C. (eds.) Hershey: IGI Global.

Hoiland, E. (2012). Neuroscience for kids. Retrieved from: http://faculty. washington.edu/chudler/plast.html.

Howard, I. P. & Templeton, W. B. (1966). *Human spatial orientation.* London: Wiley.

Hueske, E. (2011). A role for dopamine neuron NMDA receptors in learning and decision-making. Unpublished thesis, MIT. Accessed from http://hdl. handle.net/1721.1/65286.

Hutchins, E. (1996). *Cognition in the wild.* Cambridge: MIT Press.

Hutchins, E. (2000). Distributed cognition. IESBS distributed cognition. Retrieved from http://www.artmap-research.com/wp-Content/uploads/2009/11/ Hutchins_DistributedCognition.pdf. May 18, 2000.

IbHmc Clannad Man. (2008). O.J. Simpson gloves and murder trial footage. Retrieved from https://www.youtube.com/watch?v=S2YbY9eYmdM. (video file).

Jack, J. (2012). *Neurorhetorics.* New York: Psychology Press.

Jack, J. & Appelbaum, L.G. (2010). "This is your brain on rhetoric:" Research directions for neurorhetorics. *Rhetoric Society Quarterly, 40,* 411–437.

Jameson, D. A. (2004). Conceptualizing the writer-reader relationship in business prose. *Journal of Business Communication, 41,* 227–264.

Kajikawa, Y., Falchier, A., Musacchia, G., Lakatos, P., & Schroeder, C. (2012). Audiovisual integration in nonhuman primates: A window into the anatomy and physiology of cognition. In Murray, M & Wallace M. (eds.) *The neural bases of multisensory processes* (pp. 65–98). Boca Raton; CRC Press.

Kayser, C., Petkov, C. I., Remedios, R., & Logothetis, N. K. (2012). Multisensory influences on auditory processing: Perspectives from fMRI and electrophysiology. In Murray, M. & Wallace, M. (eds.) *The neural bases of multisensory processes* (pp. 99–114). Boca Raton; CRC Press.

Keetels, M. & Vroomen, J. (2012). Perception of synchrony between the senses. In Murray, M. & Wallace, M. (eds.) *The neural bases of multisensory processes* (pp. 147–177). Boca Raton; CRC Press.

Khayat P. S., Spekreijse, H., & Roelfsema, P. R. (2006). Attention lights up new object representations before the old ones fade away. *Journal of Neuroscience, 26,* 138–142. In Moore, C.I. & Cao, R. (2008). The Hemo-Neural hypothesis: On the role of blood flow in information processing. *Journal of Neurophysiology, 99,* 2035–2047.

Khoe, W., Freeman, E., Woldorff, M. G., & Mangun, G. R. (2006). Interactions between attention and perceptual grouping in human visual cortex. *Brain Res* 1078: 101–111. In Moore, C.I. & Cao, R. (2008). The hemo-neural hypothesis: On the role of blood flow in information processing. *Journal of Neurophysiology, 99,* 2035–2047.

King, A. J. & Calvert, G. (2001). Multisensory integration: Perceptual grouping by eye and ear. *Current Biology, 11,* R322–R325.

King, A. J., Doubell, T. P., & Skaliora, I. (2004). Epigentic factors that align visual and auditory maps in the ferret midbrain. In Calvert, G., Spence, C., & Stein, B. E. (eds.) *The handbook of multisensory processes* (pp. 599–612). Cambridge: MIT Press.

Klucharev, V., Smidts, A., & Fernandez, G. (2008). Brain mechanisms of persuasion: how 'expert power' modulates memory and attitudes. *SCAN, 3*, 353–366.

Kress, G. (2003). *Literacy in the new media age.* London: Routledge.

Kress, G. (2009). *Multimodality: A social semiotic approach to contemporary communication.* London: Routledge.

Kress, G. & Van Leeuwen, T. (1996; 2006). *Reading images: The grammar of visual design.* London: Routledge.

Kress, G. & Van Leeuwen, T. (2001). *Multimodal discourse: The modes and media of contemporary communication.* London: Arnold.

Krishna, A., Elder, R. S., & Caldara, C. (2010). Feminine to smell but masculine to touch?

Lacey, S. & Sathian, K. (2012). Representation of object form in vision and touch. In Murray, M. & Wallace, M. (eds.) *The neural bases of multisensory processes* (pp. 179–187). Boca Raton; CRC Press.

Landskroner Grieco Merriman, LLC. (2015). Website. www.teamlgm.com/team/attorneys/tom-merriman.

Leblanc, L. B. & Lally, C. G. (1998). A comparison of instructor-mediated versus student-mediated explicit language instruction in the communicative classroom. *The French Review, 5*, 734–746.

Lemke, J. L. (1998). Multiplying meaning: Visual and verbal semiotics in scientific text. In J. R. Martin & R. Veel (eds.) *Reading science: Critical and functional perspective on discourses of science* (pp 87–114). London: Routledge.

Lemke, J. L. (1999). Discourse and organizational dynamics: Website communication and institutional change. *Discourse and Society, 10*, 21–47.

Lewkowicz, D. J. & Kraebel, K. S. (2004). The value of multisensory redundancy in the development of intersensory perception. In Calvert, G., Spence, C., & Stein, B. E. (eds.) *The handbook of multisensory processes* (pp. 655–678). Cambridge: MIT Press.

MacDonald, E., Dadds, M., Brennan, J., Williams, K., Levy, F., & Cauchi, A. (2011). A review of safety, side-effects and subjective reactions to intranasal oxytocin in human research. *Psychoneuroendocrinology, 36*, 1114–1126.

Massumi, B. (2002). *Parables for the virtual.* Durham: Duke University Press.

Mayer, R. E. (2001). *Multi-media Learning.* Cambridge: Cambridge University Press.

Mayer, R. E. (ed.) (2005). *The Cambridge handbook of multimedia learning.* Cambridge: Cambridge UP.

Mitchell, W. J. T. (1995). *Picture theory.* Chicago: University of Chicago Press.

Moore, C. I. & Cao, R. (2008). The hemo-neural hypothesis: On the role of blood flow in information processing. *Journal of Neurophysiology, 99*, 2035–2047.

Morain, M. & Swarts, J. (2012). YouTutorial: A framework for assessing instructional online video. *Technical Communication Quarterly, 21*, 6–24.

Moreno, R. & Mayer, R. E. (2000). A learner-centered approach to multimedia explanations: Deriving instructional design principles from cognitive theory. *Interactive Multimedia Electronic Journal of Computer-Enhanced Learning, 2.*

Morrison, F. J., Bachman, H. J., & Connor, C. M. (2005). *Improving literacy in America: Guidelines from research.* New Haven, CT: Yale University Press.

Multisensory congruence and its effect on the aesthetic experience. *Journal of Consumer Psychology, 20,* 410–418.

Munhall, K. G. & Vatikiotis-Bateson, E. (2004). Spatial and temporal constraints on audiovisual speech perception. In G. Calvert, C. Spence, & B. E. Stein (eds.) *The handbook of multisensory processes* (pp. 177–188). Cambridge: MIT Press.

Murray, E. A., Sheets, H. A., & Williams, N. A. (2010). The new work of assessment: Evaluating multimodal compositions. *Computers and Composition Online.* Retrieved from http://www.bgsu.edu/cconline/murray_etal/index.html.

Murray, J. (2009). *Non-discursive Rhetoric: Image and Affect in Multimodal Composition.* New York: SUNY Press.

Murray, M. M. & Wallace, M. T. (eds.) (2012). *The neural bases of multisensory processes.* Boca Raton: CRC Press.

Nahai, Nathalie. (2012). *Webs of influence: The psychology of Online persuasion.* Harlow: Pearson.

Neal, M. (2011). *Writing assessment and the revolution in digital texts and technologies.* New York: Teachers College Press.

New London Group. (1996). A pedagogy of multiliteracies: Designing social futures. *Harvard Educational Review, 66,* 60–92.

Newell, F. N. (2004). Cross-modal object recognition. In Calvert, G., Spence, C., & Stein, B. E. (eds.) *The handbook of multisensory processes* (pp. 123–139). Cambridge: MIT Press.

Norman, D. (2004). Affordance, conventions and design. http://www.jnd.org/dn.mss/affordance_conv.html.

Norman, D. A. (1988). *The design of everyday things.* New York: Double Day.

Odell, L. & Katz, S. M. (2009). "Yes, a t-shirt!"; Assessing visual composition in the writing class. *College Composition and Communication, 61,* W197–W216.

Odell, L. & Katz, S. M. (eds.) (2012). Assessing multimedia. *Technical Communication Quarterly (special issue), 21.*

Pagonakis, J. (2015). "Tamir Rice attorney: Experts not capable of rendering independent reports on use of force" by Joe Pagonakis, posted on 10/13/2015 Retrieved from http://www.newsnet5.com/news/rice-family-attorney-questions-independent-reports-on-Odecle-police-use-of-force.

Pasqualotto, A. & Proulx, M. J. (2012). The role of visual experience for the neural basis of spatial cognition. *Neuroscience and Biobehavioral Reviews, 36,* 1179–1187.

Perelman, C. & Olbrechts-Tyteca, L. (1969). *The new rhetoric: A treatise on argumentation.* (J. Wilkinson and P. Weaver, Trans.). Notre Dame: University of Notre Dame Press.

Perrault, T. J., Rowland, B. A., & Stein, B. E. (2012). The organization and plasticity of multisensory integration on the midbrain. In Murray, M. & Wallace, M. (eds.) *The neural bases of multisensory processes* (pp. 279–300). Boca Raton; CRC Press.

Pfaff, D. & Sherman, S. (2011). Possible Legal Implications of Neural Mechanisms Underlying Ethical Behaviour. In M. Freeman (ed.) *Law and neuroscience: Current legal issues.* Volume 13. Oxford: Oxford U.P.

Pillay, S. S. (2011). Your brain and business. The neuroscience of great leaders. Upper Saddle River: Pearson/Financial Press.

Pinker, S. (1997). *How the mind works*. New York: W.W. Norton and Sons.

Popken, R. (1999). The Pedagogical Dissemination of a Genre: The Resume in American Business Discourse Textbooks, 1914–1939. *JAC: Rhetoric, Writing, Culture, Politics, 19.*

Ramsay, I. S. et al. (2013). Affective and executive network processing associated with persuasive antidrug messages. *Journal of Cognitive Neuroscience, 25*(7), 1136–47.

Reid, A. (2007). *The two virtuals: New media and composition*. West Lafayette: Parlor Press.

Remley, D. (2009). Training within industry as short-sighted community literacy-appropriate training program: A case study of a worker-centered training program. *Community Literacy Journal, 3*(2), 93–114.

Remley, D. (2010). Developing digital literacies in Second Life: Bringing Second Life to business writing pedagogy and corporate training. In W. Ritke-Jones (ed.), *Virtual environments for corporate education: Employee learning and solutions* [pp. 169–193]. Hersey, PA: IGI Global.

Remley, D. (2011). The practice of assessing multimodal PowerPoint slide shows *Computers and Composition Online*. http://www.bgsu.edu/cconline/CCpptassess/index.html.

Remley, D. (2012). Forming assessment of machinima video. *Computers and Composition Online*. Spring.

Remley, D. (2014). *Exploding technical communication: Workplace literacy hierarchies and their implications for literacy sponsorship*. Amityville: Baywood.

Remley, D. (2015). *How the brain processes multimodal technical instructions*. Amityville: Baywood.

Rentz, K. C. (1992). The value of narrative in business writing. *Journal of Business and Technical Communication, 6*, 293–315.

Rice, R. E. (1993). Media appropriateness: Using social presence theory to compare traditional and new organizational media. *Human Communication Research, 19*, 454–484.

Richards, A. R. (2003). Argument and authority in visual representations of science. *Technical Communication Quarterly, 12*, 183–206.

Rivers, N. A. (2011). Future convergences: Technical communication research as Cognitive Science. *Technical Communication Quarterly, 20*, 384–411.

Rizzolatti, G., Fadiga, L., Fogassi, L., & Gallese, V. (1996). Premotor cortex and the recognition of motor actions. *Cognitive Brain Research, 3*, 131–141.

Rodgers, P. (1989). Choice-based writing in managerial contexts: The case of the dealer contact report. *Journal of Business Communication, 23*, 197–216. http://deepblue.lib.umich.edu/bitstream/2027.42/36046/1/b1411779.0001.001.txt.

Sathian, K., Prather, S. C., & Zhang, M. (2004). Visual cortical involvement in normal tactile perception. In Calvert, G., Spence, C., & Stein, B. E. (eds) *The handbook of multisensory processes* (pp. 703–709). Cambridge: MIT Press.

Schiappa, E. (2003). *Defining reality: Definitions and the politics of meaning*. Carbondale: Southern Illinois University Press.

Schnotz, W. (2005). An integrated model of text and picture comprehension. In Mayer, R. E. (ed.) *The Cambridge handbook of multimedia learning* (pp. 49–60). Cambridge: Cambridge University Press.

Schultz, W., Apicella, P., & Ljungberg, T. (1993). Responses of monkey dopamine neurons to reward and conditioned stimuli during successive steps of learning a delayed response task. *Journal of Neuroscience, 12,* 900–913.

Shams, L., Kamitani, Y., & Shimojo, S. (2004). Modulations of visual perception by sound. In Calvert, G., Spence, C., & Stein, B. E. (eds.) *The handbook of multisensory processes* (pp. 27–33). Cambridge: MIT Press.

Shaw, G., Brown, R., & Bromiley, P. (1998). Strategic stories; How 3M is rewriting business planning. *Harvard Business Review,* May-June. Retrieved from https://hbr.org/1998/05/strategic-stories-how-3m-is-rewriting-business-planning.

Sheridan, D. M., Ridolfo, J., & Michel, A. J. (2012). *The available means of persuasion: Mapping a theory and pedagogy of multimodal public rhetoric.* Anderson: Parlor Press.

Simons, H. W. & Jones, J. (2011). *Persuasion in society.* New York: Taylor and Francis.

Sorapure, M. (2005). Between modes: Assessing student new media compositions. *Kairos, 10*(2).

Spence, C., Parise, C., & Chen, Y. (2012). The Colavita visual dominance effect. In Murray, M. & Wallace, M. (eds.). *The neural bases of multisensory processes* (pp. 529–556). Boca Raton; CRC Press.

Teston, C. (2012). Moving from artifact to action: A grounded investigation of visual displays of evidence during medical deliberations. *Technical Communication Quarterly, 21,* 187–209.

Toulmin, S. (2003). *Uses of argument.* Cambridge: Cambridge University Press (original work published in 1958).

Tufte, E. R. (1990). *Envisioning information.* Cheshire: Graphics Press.

Tufte, E. R. (2003). *The cognitive style of PowerPoint.* Cheshire, CT: Graphics Press.

Tufte, E. R. (2006). *Beautiful evidence.* Graphics Press.

Turing, A. M. (1950). Computing machinery and intelligence. *Mind Quarterly Review Psychological Philosophy, 59,* 433–460.

Van Horn, J. et al. (2012). Mapping connectivity damage in the case of Phineas Gage. *PLoS One* 16 May 2012.

van Leeuwen, T. (2003). A multimodal perspective on composition in Ensink, T. & Sauer, C. (eds.) *Framing and perspectivising in discourse,* Amsterdam, Benjamins.

Venton, B. J., Seipel, A. T., Phillips, P. E., Wetsel, W. C., Gitler, D., Greengard, P. et al. (2006). Cocaine increases dopamine release by mobilization of a synapsin-dependent reserve pool. *Journal of Neuroscience, 26,* 3206–3209.

Volkow, N. D., Wang, G. J., Telang, F., Fowler, J. S., Logan, J., Jayne, M., Ma, Y., Pradhan, K., & Wong, C. (2007). Profound decreases in dopamine release in striatum in detoxified alcoholics: possible orbitofrontal involvement. *Journal of Neuroscience,* Nov 14; 27(46), 12700–6.

Vygotsky, L. (1978). *Mind in society; The development of higher psychological processes.* M. Cole, S. Scribner, V. John-Steiner, & E. Souberman (eds.). Cambridge: Harvard U. P.

Vygotsky, L. (1986). *Thought and language.* Cambridge, MA: MIT Press.

Wallace, M. T. (2004). The development of multisensory integration. In Calvert, G., Spence, C., & Stein, B. E. (eds.) *The handbook of multisensory processes* (pp. 625–642). Cambridge: MIT Press.

Wallace, M. T., Perrault, T. J. Jr., Hairston, W. D. & Stein, B. E. (2004). Visual experience is necessary for the development of multisensory integration. *The Journal of Neuroscience, 27*, 9580–9584.

Whithaus, C. (2012). Claim-evidence structures in environmental science writing: Modifying Toulmin's model to account for multimodal arguments. *Technical Communication Quarterly, 21*, 105–128.

Welch, R. & Warren, D. (1986). Intersensory interactions. In. Boff, K., Kauffman, L., & Thomas, J. (eds.) *Handbook of perception and human performance: Vol I. Sensory processes and human performance.* New York: Wiley.

Worden, M. S., Foxe J. J., Wang, N., & Simpson, G.V. (2000). Anticipatory biasing of visuospatial attention indexed by retinotopically specific alpha-band electroencephalography increases over occipital cortex. *Journal of Neuroscience* 20: RC63. In Moore, C. I. & Cao, R. (2008). The hemo-neural hypothesis: On the role of blood flow in information processing. *Journal of Neurophysiology, 99*, 2035–2047.

Ziemer Andrews, K. L. (2007). The effects of implicit and explicit instruction on simple and complex grammatical structures for adult language learners. *Teaching English as a Second Language-EJ, 11.2*, 1–15.

Index

Printed in the United States
by Baker & Taylor Publisher Services